Plug in Your Life

Living a Fulfilling Life while in Pursuit of Your Meaningful Goals and Dreams

Hunter Kallay

WESTBOW PRESS®
A DIVISION OF THOMAS NELSON & ZONDERVAN

This book is a work of non-fiction. Unless otherwise noted, the author and the publisher make no explicit guarantees as to the accuracy of the information contained in this book and in some cases, names of people and places have been altered to protect their privacy.

WestBow Press books may be ordered through booksellers or by contacting:

WestBow Press
A Division of Thomas Nelson & Zondervan
1663 Liberty Drive
Bloomington, IN 47403
www.westbowpress.com
1 (866) 928-1240

ISBN: 978-1-5127-0780-9 (sc)
ISBN: 978-1-5127-0781-6 (hc)
ISBN: 978-1-5127-0779-3 (e)

Library of Congress Control Number: 2015913002

Print information available on the last page.

WestBow Press rev. date: 09/01/2015

Contents

This book is dedicated to my family.
I love you all.

Preface

Anyone who holds on to life just as it is destroys that life. But if you let it go, reckless in your love, you'll have it forever, real and eternal.
—John 12:25 MSG

Fulfillment in life is not determined by the trophies that you win, the publicity or money that you acquire, or your social status. Fulfillment comes from your relationship with God and openly letting His Will be done through you. That is where true greatness is born.

Life is difficult sometimes, and life is pleasing sometimes. We have all experienced both the favorable and detestable sides of life. In this book, I hope to help you better understand how God is constantly working in your life and how to deal with the situations that He gives you. The purpose of this book is to guide you in allowing God to take complete control of your life and letting His Will be done through your goals and dreams.

We all might say that we want what is best for us, but really, most of us just want what *we* want, and what *we* think will provide us fulfillment and pleasure in life. Plugging in your life is an idea I came up with that basically means willingly letting God provide you with all that He has in store for your life, without restrictions. This is done by living in response to what Jesus has done for you on the cross.

Sometimes we will let God do all that He wants ... except take our jobs away, or put us through pain. Those are just basic examples. Everyone craves control, and giving up things to God that are so important to us can be difficult. However, giving God everything is the only way to live a life fulfilling your true eternal purpose and to live a life of true joy and contentment.

God wants *all* of you. He loves your good and bad qualities unconditionally. Do not put limits on what God can do. His plan for you is better than anything you could ever dream of or imagine.

Your life is like a puzzle, and you must give God all of the pieces in order to get the full, beautifully fulfilled picture. You possess all the pieces of your puzzle—good and bad, that you don't really know how to position. You have a certain addiction/talent/passion/friend/etc.—all are pieces of your puzzle that you don't quite know how to put together. God wants to put that puzzle together in your life. If you only give God the good pieces of your life and hide your bad things from Him, trying to fix them on your own before you give yourself fully up to His plan, then God won't be able to build the full puzzle—you won't have a full life. But if you give the Lord everything, He will show you the beautiful plugged in life that He desires for you.

Fear can control us, but only if we let it. We sometimes say things like, "God can put me through anything except ..." and finish with something that we are afraid of. The problem is, if you live within a comfort bubble, it will eventually pop.

The LORD is my light and my salvation—whom shall I fear? The LORD is the stronghold of my life—of whom shall I be afraid?
—Psalm 27:1 NIV

God doesn't want half of you and not all but one or two things. God wants everything. Do not be ashamed of your negative actions and think that you will give yourself up to God once you get your life together, because your life will never be perfect in your own eyes; however, God wants the negative, sinful things about you just as much as He wants the positive things. God wants to use your positive and negative traits for His perfect plan. He wants to turn your sins into blessings and demonstrations of His Love. God gave His only Son to die for *you* so that *you* could have a relationship with Him even though you are imperfect. It is because of what Jesus did on the cross that you can plug in your life to Him. God doesn't want you to get down on yourself when you sin and mess up over and over. Instead, He wants you to give your sins up to Him so that He can perfectly use them for the good. When you give up your bad habits, painful addictions, and hurtful relationships to God, He will recycle those things and use them in His perfect plan for you.

I was inspired to write this book because I love to read, and my dream was to eventually write my own book with my own ideas on life. I am very passionate about living life for God and living with a purpose. I believe that there should be purpose behind every action—especially behind your goals and dreams. In life, we all want to accomplish certain goals, but sometimes we put them off until the perfect opportunity comes, and it never will—it must be *created*.

When I was writing this book, I only told few people what I was doing until it was finished because I didn't want to hear how hard it was going to be. I didn't want to hear anything that would fill me with doubt, and I didn't want to hear how I should wait until I am older to write it. I also didn't want to tell everyone because then the book would be all about me and my accomplishment of writing a book.

People might say that it is admirable to write and publish a book at the age of sixteen; however, I don't want this book to be about me, because it's not. This book is for the glory of God and to inspire people to live lives of meaning and fulfillment.

My hope for this book is that you learn the principles and consider the ideas for your life that are presented and explained in it. Throughout this book, I want to show you the importance of making the most of every moment as well as guide you in chasing your goals and dreams. I also want to teach you the importance of living your life out of love, demonstrate how to do that, and help edify your life.

I hope that you don't just learn the principles and ideas in this book, but that you apply them to your life in order to live a fulfilling life and to live out God's purpose for you. Sometimes life is confusing because we have these passions and desires to do great things but we don't know what to do with them until our lives are plugged into God's Will. This book will help get you started on that journey.

My hope for you is that you will be inspired to live with God as the center of your life and develop into the best version of yourself as you read each page of this book.

A pretentious, showy life is an empty life; a
plain and simple life is a full life.
—Proverbs 13:7-9 MSG

1

The Outlet

It's in Christ that we find out who we are and what we are living for. Long before we first heard of Christ and got our hopes up, He had his eye on us, had designs on us for glorious living, part of the overall purpose He is working out in everything and everyone.
—Ephesians 1:11 MSG

Imagine the greatest life that you could ever live. Imagine having the best job, the best house, the best family, the perfect spouse, and ultimate fulfillment and happiness in your life. Doesn't that sound awesome? It sure does to me! Now what if I told you that there was better?

God has a plan in store for your life that is greater than any plan you could ever imagine, because He knows exactly what will bring you true fulfillment in life. I call this life *the plugged in life*.

God's plan is accessed by plugging in your life to His perfect Will. Plugging in your life means giving up absolutely everything in order to live out the life that God has in store—the plugged in life. Living a plugged in life doesn't mean to be passive and rely on God for everything, but instead to be submissive and willing to *do* all that He wants you to do. I like what Mark Batterson says in his book, *All In*. He says, "The Will of God is not an insurance plan. It's a daring plan." Plugging in your life means to go all in with your dreams and your faith. We are all designed to live out God's plan for our lives, but what most of us lack is the ability to make the necessary sacrifices for it. Plugging in your life is not all about *buying in*; it is also about *selling out*. The plugged in life takes hard work and sacrifice, and it all starts with a solid foundation.

Your Foundation

What is the foundation of your life? What holds your life together? What could you not live without? Your foundation controls everything in your life. If you have a strong foundation, you can build a strong life. If you have a weak foundation, your life will crumble down.

Imagine the foundation of a skyscraper. If a skyscraper has a foundation made of pebbles, not much can be built on it. If it has a foundation of sand, it will be uneven and crumble down. However, if that foundation is made of something strong and supportive, that building can be built tall, and the foundation can bear as much as it needs to.

In order to live the plugged in life, your foundation must be your relationship with God. When your relationship with God is the foundation of your life, you can build whatever will praise Him on top.

Let's say you are trying to put on muscle. You reduce your fat content, eat less sugar, and increase your protein intake. On top of that, you drink protein shakes, take pre-workout, and use all different kinds of supplements to aid you in building muscle. However, if you don't lift weights or work out, you simply aren't going to build the muscle that you desire.

In that example, lifting weights is the foundation. With no foundation, everything else that you do is meaningless.

In life, doing what God wants is your weight lifting—everything else is supplementary. You can say you are a Christian and can go to church, pray, and read the Bible, but if you don't have ultimate faith in God and a trusting relationship with Him, you are missing the foundation to fulfillment. You, as a sinner, will always have cracks in your foundation—some things that you do wrong—but God's Love for you through Jesus Christ is what fills in those cracks.

The Wise and Foolish Builders

Therefore everyone who hears these words of Mine and puts them into practice is like a wise man who built his house on the rock. The rain came down, the streams rose, and the winds blew and beat against that house; yet it did not fall, because it had its foundation on the rock. But everyone who hears these words of Mine and does not put them into practice is like a foolish man who built his house on sand.

The rain came down, the streams rose, and the winds blew and beat against that house, and it fell with a great crash.
—Matthew 7:24–27 NIV

Plugging in your life is living in response to God's Love for you through Jesus Christ. You can't have a half-plugged in life. Jesus made no compromises when He gave His life for you, and He takes no compromises when He asks you to plug in your life.

God is the electrical outlet to your life. You are like a phone, a computer, a TV—something that is extraordinary. You have all of this potential to do wonderful things, but you aren't at your full potential, living a life of fulfillment, because you aren't plugged in! When you plug your life into that electrical outlet—when you plug your life into God's Will—a special connection is made, and you will be turned on and fully able to be used by God so that your potential can flourish.

An unplugged TV is meaningless. It is not enjoyable, and there is no power shining through. Your life is the same way. God is the power that controls your life. You can change the channel—change what you do—but that is only possible because of God's power—the electricity. You have the free will to express God's Grace in your life in all different ways through your talents and abilities, but it is all because of Him and for His glory. Don't live a meaningless life; live one of purpose and direction. Live a life guided by God. The change in your life will be as dramatic as a TV being plugged in—it will be that noticeable.

If you remain unplugged, like a smartphone without energy or charge, you cannot be used and your life is meaningless. When you charge your phone by plugging it in, you are giving it the power and energy that allows it to operate. You can then use that phone to do what you want, but it is all because you plugged it in—it is powered by that electricity.

Plugging in your life is a commitment, but it is not a trap. Letting God's Will be done in your life does not mean your joy is lost; it means your joy is found. You can do what you want and enjoy the pleasures of life, but within the boundaries of what God knows is good for you.

Sometimes we think that by doing certain things, we will be fulfilled and have true joy. We often think thoughts like, *Once I get that degree/job/truck/financial status, I will have joy*. Then we get those things and are jubilant, but that happiness eventually wears off, and we still aren't living a joyful, fulfilling life. Contentment is essential to fulfillment in life, and without God manning the control center of your life, contentment is a moving target.

Stop enduring your life and start enjoying it. You can't live in potential for the rest of your life. At some point, things have to change—*you* have to change. God has blessed you with talents, gifts, opportunities, and all other elements in life needed to praise Him through fulfilling His purpose for you. All of this leads to one question: How do I plug in my life?

In the ensuing chapters of this book, I will answer that question. I will explain how to plug in your life and stay plugged in, so that you can live a fulfilling life. There is something more to your life, and it is only found through plugging into God.

Fulfill is defined by Dictionary.com as "1. to carry out, or bring to realization, as a prophesy or promise. 2. to perform or do, as duty; obey or follow, as commands … 5. to develop the full potential of." Fulfillment in life means carrying out and bringing to realization God's prophesy and promise for your life. It means obeying what He says, living life God's way instead of your own way.

You must fulfill in order to be fulfilled; meaning, you must fulfill God's plan for you and pray over His promises in order to develop into your full potential. God is waiting for your permission to bring purpose into your life. When will you decide to give Him that?

> *The degree to which we surrender control is the degree to which we will benefit in this life and in the life to come.*
> —*Andy Stanley,* Louder than Words

Pastor Rick Warren explains that there are three barriers that keep us from surrendering our lives to God:

1. Fear
2. Pride
3. Confusion

Fear

Fear causes us to be scared of what will happen to our comfortable lives if we let God take over. Some people are just scared that all of the things that they love might be taken away, and their comfortable lives will become discombobulated. You become whole in spirit when you accept God's favor fully in your life. The faith to surrender your life to God breeds the faith to continue the journey.

Pride

Pride is what keeps us thinking that we can provide a fulfilling life for ourselves.

Everyone has a feeling of emptiness inside of them—a feeling that they want to own or control something. Everyone wants at least one thing to call theirs, whether that is a certain person, activity, possession, or something else. I call that thing their *pride spot*.

For example, if a kid is made fun of in gym class, he might not care. He might just make fun of himself and say how bad of an athlete he is; however, if he plays the drums and someone tells him that he isn't good at playing the drums, then he will get defensive. That is because he feels ownership over playing the drums. That is his pride spot.

We all have a sense of pride that we don't want to give up. We want control over things, and that's almost become part of human nature.

Pride goes before destruction, a haughty spirit before a fall.
—Proverbs 16:18 NIV

Confusion

Some people are just confused about where they are on their faith journey. They are confused about where to start and who God is. Why would you want a stranger to take control of everything in your life and give up all that you love to them? Some people who see Jesus as a stranger may hesitate to give Him complete control. The way to solve this confusion is to learn about Jesus and His teachings and also learn about God's Grace and how much He loves you. Once you have an intimate relationship with God and love Him with all your heart, mind, soul, and strength, it is more natural for you to understand the purpose of giving up your life to His Will. Also, the more you understand the Power of God, the more desire you will have to let God's Will be done in your life because you know that He will do unprecedented things through you. Plugging in your life is a matter of loving God more than you love any of the things or people of this life.

In Luke 14:26, Jesus says, *"If anyone comes to Me and does not hate his own father and mother and wife and children and brothers and sisters, yes, and even his own life, he cannot be My disciple." (ESV)* Jesus is very blunt here in what it means to plug in your life to Him. The word "hate" in this passage has roots in Attic Greek that mean to "love less," or to "separate or remove one's self from entangling relationships or circumstances which might come between the disciple and the master." Jesus is simply saying that you must not let even your family or any other thing in your life get between Him and you. The New Living Translation says, "...you must hate everyone else by comparison." Plugging in your life means to love God more than anyone or anything in this world—including your own life.

> *Do not offer any part of yourself to sin as an instrument of wickedness, but rather offer yourselves to God as those who have been brought from death to life; and offer every part of yourself to Him as an instrument of righteousness.*
> —*Romans 6:13 NIV*

In Touch Ministries *(http://www.intouch.org)* describes 22 promises that God has made us in the Bible. There are more than 3000 of God's promises in Scripture, but all of His promises are the basis for our lives, and they are all guarantees if you plug in your life to Him and pray over them.

1. Our reconciliation to God through the death of Christ
   —Romans 5:6-10
2. The daily forgiveness of our sins
   —1 John 1:9
3. The Father's continued presence wherever we go
   —Deuteronomy 31:8
4. A constant Helper through the in-dwelling presence of the Holy Spirit
   —John 14:16

5. The Lord's strength in whatever diffi-culty we face
—Isaiah 41:10
6. God's provision for our daily needs
—Matthew 6:25-32
7. An answer to our prayers
—1 John 5:14-15
8. The Lord's supply of blessing
—Psalm 84:11
9. The Father's daily help with our burdens.
—Psalm 68:19
10. God's comfort in our distress
—2 Corinthians 1:3-4
11. A way of escape when we are tempted
—1 Corinthians 10:13
12. Wisdom for every challenge
—James 1:5
13. Rest for our weary souls
—Matthew 11:28-29
14. Peace regardless of the troubles we face
—Philippians 4:6-7
15. Fruitfulness as we grow older
—Psalm 92:12-15
16. The desires of our hearts
—Psalm 37:4
17. Help in times of trouble
—Psalm 46:1-3
18. Guidance along the pathway of life
—Psalm 32:8

19. Healing for our diseases and wounds
—Psalm 103:1-3
20. The absolute guarantee of God's Love
—Romans 8:38-39
21. Eternal security
—John 10:27-30
22. Heaven as our eternal home
—John 14:1-3

The Creator of the universe has *promised* you all of these things and much more! He has a purpose for your life. By plugging in your life, you are bringing to realization God's promises for your life. *All* of these promises are fulfilled by plugging in your life to God.

The Want Factor

In order to plug in your life, you must *want* God's plan for your life. You must *want* change. If you don't want to achieve a goal deep in your heart, then you will burn out down the road to achieving it. It is the same with plugging in your life and living for God, entirely His way. The more you learn about God, the more desire you will have to let His Will be done in your life.

You are a computer with unlimited potential to help others and have God's Power shine through you so that you can bring glory to Him through the talents and abilities He gave you. Sometimes we make the mistake that we think we know what we need and where we are supposed to go. The truth is, only God knows those things. Plugging in your life means letting God take the wheel.

Are you ready to give up the driver's seat and let God drive the car of your life? He will drive you down roads that you didn't even know existed and take you to places better than you could ever imagine. Get ready, because this journey will change your life and enhance the way you live. Live your life fulfilled. Plug in your life. Light does not shine through an unplugged lamp.

2

Living Out of Love

We know that we have passed from death to life, because we love each other. Anyone who does not love remains in death.
—1 John 3:14 NIV

In a *TED Talks* seminar, Anthony Robbins explains that fulfillment is derived from three main areas: growth, appreciation, and contribution. Don't you feel good when you see improvement? Don't you feel good when you take time out of your busy life to admire a beautiful view? Don't you feel good when you act out of benevolence and help someone with something? Those moments of growth, contribution, and appreciation are feelings of brief fulfillment. All three of these things surround one central feeling: love. If you can learn how to live your life out of love, then those feelings of fulfillment will invigorate all that you do.

Love is the key to fulfillment. There are six principles that are essential to live a life of true fulfillment by living out of love.

1. Accept God's Love
2. Love yourself
3. Give love
4. Receive love
5. Do what you love
6. Appreciate love

If you master living your life out of these six principles, then you will be on your way to living a life of true fulfillment, and everything that you do will have more purpose and meaning.

Three things will last forever—faith, hope, and love—and the greatest of these is love.
—1 Corinthians 13:13 NLT

1. Accept God's Love

No eye has seen, no ear has heard, and no mind has imagined what God has prepared for those who love Him.
—1 Corinthians 2:9 NLT

God is simply love Himself. His Love is perpetual. God loves *you* no matter what. When God loves, it is not an action. God is simply love itself. When God loves you, He is simply being Himself—He is being love. God's Love for you is unconditional and infinite because God is infinite, therefore, so is His Love.

Knowing that God loves you unconditionally is a big step of faith. So many of us make mistakes in life, have doubts about our beliefs that we feel guilty about, curse God, and think that we are going to Hell because of it. Who is to judge that but God Himself, who loves you unconditionally? *Unconditional* is defined by Dictionary.com as, "not limited by conditions; absolute." God's Love for *you* is absolute; meaning that no matter what, under any condition, He loves you to an extent that none of us can comprehend.

Romans 8:31 says that God is *for* you, not against you. Everything that God does is for your good to promote you to fulfill your purpose that He has given you. If you know that every setback in your life is actually a blessing *for* you, then you are accepting God's Love. Knowing this will take away your unneeded worries and give you contentment through His Grace and Mercy.

1 John 4:19 says, "*We love because He first loved us.*" *(NIV)* Living out of love is living in response to God's Love for you. Through this authentic response, all of the six principles of living out of love are followed. This whole book is all just a simplified guide to living out an authentic response to God's Love for you. No matter how much you turn against Him or choose to submit to your flesh, God's Love for you never changes. Fulfillment in life is found by living in response to God's Love. By living out of love this way, the positive and negative of your past, present, and future will all be shaped and directed into God's perfect plan for your life.

Sometimes we can see God acting in our lives and other times He seems to be missing. Most of us have had an experience in life, maybe many, in which we thought to ourselves, *that must've been an act of God.* There are some things in our lives that we just cannot explain. Those moments are incredible. Then, there are times when our lives are falling apart and we feel alone. Sometimes God is letting you go through a struggle so that He can mold you into the person that you need to be in order to handle His plethora of favor in your future. God will not let anything happen to you that He doesn't intend to happen. He never makes a mistake.

> *We can rejoice, too, when we run into problems and trials, for we know that they help us develop endurance. And endurance develops strength of character, and character strengthens our confident hope of salvation. And this hope will not lead to disappointment. For we know how dearly God loves us, because He has given us the Holy Spirit to fill our hearts with His Love.*
> *—Romans 5:3-5 NLT*

In the book, *Chicken Soup for the Soul,* author and motivational speaker Jack Canfield says, "When driving at night from California to New York, you don't need to see all the way from one coast to another. All you need is for your headlights to show you the next two hundred feet in front, and you will get there. In life, you have to trust that you will be 'shown the way.'" Most people, he observes, never ask for what they want because they cannot see *how* it could possibly come to them.

What Canfield describes in this analogy is the perfect example of how we need to trust in God. You may not see the whole picture of how you will get through an obstacle to your success or why God is taking you a certain route. Plugging in your life means to go as far as you know to go, as far as you can see, and then trust God to show you the next two hundred feet. Paul says in 2 Corinthians 5:7, *"For we live by faith, not by sight." (NIV)*

By the Grace of God, He will show you and lead you to the destination He has in store for you. Plugging in your life means acting out in your faith by doing what you know you must do and abiding by God's lead. It is through faith this faith that you begin to find fulfillment in life.

I don't want your sacrifices—I want your love; I don't want your offerings—I want you to know Me.
—Hosea 6:6 TLB

God gave His only begotten Son to die the most humbling of deaths so that you could have a relationship with Him. In order to develop that relationship with God, you must learn to trust Him. Trust is needed in order to love, and you can trust God because He has never failed anyone, ever. Peace is found when you trust in God and remember His sovereignty over every situation.

Jesus replied: "Love the LORD your God with all your heart and with all your soul and with all your mind." This is the first and greatest commandment.
—Matthew 22:37-38 NIV

2/3/4. The Cycle of Love

Loving who you are, giving love, and receiving love all go hand in hand. One cannot exist without the others. I call this *The Cycle of Love*. In order to love others fully and passionately, you must love yourself. If you don't love yourself, then how can you truly love others? That doesn't mean to adore yourself and think that you are better than anyone else. It simply means to be proud of who you are and love who God has created you to be, the way that He did. Giving in to temptation and being a sinner doesn't mean you should think less of yourself, you just have to think of yourself less and think of God's Love more. God created you perfectly to fulfill your purpose, so when you don't love who you are, you are saying that what God has made is imperfect.

Each morning, I challenge you to take time to appreciate one thing about yourself that makes you unique. Throughout the day, focus on that thing and learn to appreciate it. You cannot experience true fulfillment if you don't love yourself.

How much we know and understand ourselves is critically important, but there is something that is even more essential to a wholehearted life: loving ourselves.
—Brene Brown, The Gifts of Imperfection

Think of someone that loves you. This might be a family member, a friend, your spouse, anyone. No matter who you are, you have people who love you in your life. Learn to recognize that love more often and embrace that love. When you are around someone who loves you, you feel good. Don't be afraid to let that feeling overwhelm you. Love is the most powerful feeling in the world, so don't minimize it or shy away from it.

Love should be one of the most valued things in your life, if not, the most valued. Feeling love is feeling fulfillment. The desire to feel loved by people is in all of our hearts. Therefore, when we receive this love and just let it flow through us, our hearts are filled with true joy.

When you love yourself, giving love to others is effortless. Imagine a glass that is being filled up with water. The water represents love being given to you by people, and the size of the glass represents the size of your love for yourself. The more love that you have for yourself, the bigger the glass is. As you let water pour into the glass, eventually, the glass fills up, starts to overflow, and then it begins to pour over the sides. As long as water is still being poured into the glass, water keeps overflowing.

This is a simple metaphor to understand. When you love yourself enough to receive love, it will flow through you and out of you, and you will begin to increasingly notice the feeling of fulfillment that it brings. This is simply living out of love. Water cannot fill the glass if there is no glass, and if the glass is tiny, not much love can be given; therefore, you cannot truly receive love to its fullest if you don't love yourself. When you don't love all that God has made you to be, you cannot give love to your full potential either. Living a fulfilling life all starts with loving yourself. God is love, and He has given us the ability to love, so He is glorified and praised when you love yourself and when we, His children, love each other.

You owe everyone in this world the expression of love. Every time you approach somebody, remember to show love by wishing no harm on them and making their lives easier any way that doesn't harm yours. Live with a sense of *eagerness* to express love.

Accept one another, then, just as Christ accepted you, in order to bring praise to God.
—Romans 15:7 NIV

5. Do What You Love

It's not what you do, but how much love you put into it that matters.
—Mother Teresa

Doing things that we love brings us joy. It's that simple sometimes. When you do those things that you love doing, you are again, living out of love.

Many of us try to do things that we don't enjoy so that we can acquire money and/or publicity. When we take this route, we most often wear down and burn out. When you do things that you love, you are instead living joyfully and allowing God to work through your inspired actions rather than forcing your own action. Forced action is what causes us to burn out because our work seems tedious and we don't enjoy it. Love inspires and drives passion. Simply put, you will be passionate about the things that you love.

Have you ever gotten so caught up in doing something that you love and then when you finish, you look back and notice that you have gotten a ton of work done even though you didn't seem to put forth much effort? That is because you were living out of love, so the action seemed effortless rather than menial. That is inspired action. Inspired action is a gift from God that makes following our passion fulfilling.

Avoid traps that will steer you away from fulfillment. That means, avoid situations and people that don't bring you joy. If that means limiting time with a friend that is not healthy for you or even quitting an unhealthy job, then that's what you have to do in order to find fulfillment in your life. Don't do things just for the joy of others if it is hurting you, because that will leave you empty on the inside and cause you to burn out. Instead, do things that you love and enjoy and let your joy and efforts pour out onto others to make a difference in the world.

And this is love: that we walk in obedience to His commands. As you have heard from the beginning, His command is that you walk in love.
—2 John 1:6 NIV

6. Appreciate love

When you see someone hold the door for someone else, donate money, or do a good deed, take time to appreciate that. Generosity that comes from the heart is a form of love. If you see big acts of generosity happening in the world, or even little acts, make a habit of appreciating them and let them fill you with feelings of love and bliss.

When a happy couple walks by and you see the passion in their eyes, appreciate their love for each other. Let that love make you feel happy and fill you with joy. Appreciate the good things in this world and the kind hearts.

Appreciating love will bring you more joy and make you feel more love for the things and people around you. You will begin to see this world from a whole new perspective once you begin appreciating love.

Above all, clothe yourselves with love, which
binds us all together in perfect harmony.
—Colossians 3:14 NLT

Time

Time is the most valuable resource that we have on this earth because it produces possibility and opportunity. Time cannot be found, it must be made. You cannot "find time" to do something, you must *make* time to do it. When you love others, the greatest gift you can give them is your time. When you can sacrifice a little extra time to show and appreciate love, your life will be permeated with joy.

You will make time for those things and people that you love, and you will simply find more important "things" to do with your time if you don't truly love them. Time is the sacrifice that measures your love for something. The more you love someone or something, the more time you will desire to invest into that person or thing.

You might have heard the expression, "Time stops when I'm with you." You start to truly love when time stops getting in the way of what you are doing. Love is what this world revolves around. Love is the engine to life. If you are willing to give up your valuable time for someone or something else, then you are truly able to live out of love.

Operation Complete

Love is the most powerful force and feeling in the universe. If you use this to your advantage and are passionate about love itself, then your life will change dramatically, and fulfillment will be in your midst.

Love is an eternal emotion. It comes from deep in the heart and in the spirit. It touches your eternal being and soul. Everything, and I do mean everything, revolves around love.

The Way of Love

If I speak with human eloquence and angelic ecstasy but don't love, I'm nothing but the creaking of a rusty gate.

If I speak God's Word with power, revealing all His mysteries and making everything plain as day, and if I have faith that says to a mountain, "Jump," and it jumps, but I don't love, I'm nothing.

If I give everything I own to the poor and even go to the stake to be burned as a martyr, but I don't love, I've gotten nowhere. So, no matter what I say, what I believe, and what I do, I'm bankrupt without love.
—1 Corinthians 13:1-7 MSG

3

Brain Matching

How do you adjust or alter your mindset so that you can be plugged into the plan God has for your life? You can probably think of at least few things or maybe many areas of your life that you know you need to work on in order to give your life fully up to God. Brain Matching is an effective technique that can be used to liberate you from negative areas of your life and aid you in plugging in your life to God's purpose for you.

The basis for how our minds work and how we can experience life to the fullest is through the basic concept of Brain Matching. Brain Matching is a protective axiom or idea. Learning this idea could be pivotal in how you think and how you live your life. Understanding Brain Matches and how to use them will help you have the right thought process throughout the applying process of this book and also help you to understand the beauty of your own thoughts.

Brain Matches are simply associations that we make in our mind. In the past, you might have heard someone say that they associate a positive or negative feeling with something or someone based on a past experience, but actually, we associate *everything* we do in life and every person that we meet with a feeling or a result. This feeling or result can be positive or negative and it can be changed if we intentionally work on changing it. Although we Brain Match everything in life, the Brain Matches we create are a choice that we have. We develop all of our Brain Matches and therefore we have the power to control and alter them. Brain Matches are the cause of fears, passions, things we enjoy, things we hate, and how we feel about everything. These associations are emotional, physical, spiritual, and mental.

Brain Matches are all self-created. Brain Matching can be done both consciously and unconsciously. However, you can always become aware of them. You can change every aspect of your life including school, eating habits, losing weight, training, motivation, success, addictions, and any little thing that you want if you understand this concept of Brain Matching and how to use it to deliberately change your thought process any way you desire.

Have you ever wondered why you dread working out? Why you naturally crave junk foods, and not healthy foods? How you can change an unwanted habit? Why do you want to lose weight but don't have a burning desire to go to the gym? Do you drag yourself to the gym, or does the gym give you a sense of happiness? Why do you get upset when things don't go as planned, and what is the actual reason behind loving and fearing surprises? Why do you fear what you fear? All of these questions can be answered, your feelings and the way you live your life will be understood, and your thoughts will be under your own control if you understand and master the idea of Brain Matching.

The most effective way to explain Brain Matching is through example and through relatable thoughts and situations in life. Throughout this chapter, you will begin to understand Brain Matches and how they can be used to change your life through real life examples.

Brain Matching is referenced throughout this book and is a concept that will change the way you think about a lot of things, and it will also give you a different perspective on how your mind works. Understanding Brain Matching will also guide you in taking a different and more pure perspective on events, circumstances, places, and people throughout the rest of your life to aid you in following God's plan for your life.

Brain Matches From Previous Experience

Have you ever seen someone jump to their phone as soon as an alert for a text message or email goes off? Do you get a strong urge to check your phone when you feel the vibration? If you answered yes to one or both of these questions, it's due to Brain Matching.

As humans, we all have a natural craving to feel appreciated. When people "like" our post on Facebook, we feel that pleasing feeling. Our previous experiences determine a lot about how we feel about certain endeavors that we currently have every single day.

In the past, you may have gotten texts or notifications that made you feel good or appreciated. You jump to your phone when you feel it vibrate because you associate that vibration with a good feeling that you have had in the past. In the past, maybe you have gotten a "like" on a Facebook status, Instagram post, or a text message from a friend that made you feel good. You then match up the feeling that you had when you saw those things to the vibration or ring of your phone; so when your phone goes off, you crave that feeling and check your phone. Then, when you check your phone and see a pleasing text message that you were sent, you feel that good feeling that you desired and your Brain Match is strengthened.

"RING!" = Pleasing Feeling

For example, a salesperson is always going straight to his/her phone when it vibrates or rings because he/she associates that ring with a sale, in turn, money. A ring might be matched in their brain with money because of past experiences of getting sales over phone calls.

"RING!" = Sale = Money
THEREFORE
"RING!" = Money

On our way to Texas one summer, my dad went to change lanes on the interstate and heard a loud honk. He couldn't see the driver in his blind spot coming up on his left side. The next time my dad went to change lanes, he made sure he double checked to see if a car was in his blind spot. That is simply Brain Matching a past experience.

Changing lanes = "HONK!"
DEVELOPS
Changing lanes = Driver in blind spot

My grandparents were over at my house one day and I was talking to them about a recent trip that I went on. I went to offer my papa some Indian food, and he quickly declined, almost as if he was afraid of it. He then went on to tell me about how he and his Lebanese fraternity brother had Indian food in Florida back when he was in college. He said that everybody raved about it in the area so they tried it. Long story short, it made him get very sick. Many years later, my papa still Brain Matches Indian food with getting sick. His Brain Match has never changed.

These Brain Matches that are based on past experience can also be a cause of fear. Sometimes our fears come from past experiences without us even knowing it.

Maybe you are afraid of water, and you don't even know why. It could be something as simple as you fell in a pond when you were little and choked on the water a little bit. That can be a startling feeling, especially at a young age. Ever since that moment, you could be unconsciously associating water with that startling feeling that you have felt in the past. Then, when people ask you why you are afraid, you just say that you honestly don't know. That is because you might have forgotten the event, but you've grown accustomed to that Brain Match always being there.

Water = Startling feeling from falling in at young age

Like with my papa and Indian food, Brain Matches don't wear out over time. They exist the way they do until a similar experience produces a different feeling or result. This is why "facing your fears" works sometimes—it changes your Brain Match if the experience produces a different result. I'm not saying that if you don't know why you fear something, it is all definitely based on a past experience. For example, your fear could simply exist because you created a Brain Match of water and drowning; however, you can overcome any fear by changing your Brain Matches. Instead of being afraid of drowning every time you see water, focus on fun times that water has the potential to bring. Every time you see water, think of things like tubing, boating with friends, shelling, fishing, playing in the waves with your family, and deliberately focus on changing the association that is in your head. As you do this more often, you will start to feel better about your fear and it will become habit for you to think of fun every time you see water.

Water = Drowning
DELIBRATELY CHANGED TO
Water = Fun

This method isn't just applied to a fear of water; it can help you to overcome any fear. Whether it's physical or emotional, all fears are self-imposed. That means that you create them in your mind. Since you create your own fears, you can overcome them as well. You are only born with two fears: falling and loud noises. All others are self-created.

Brain Matching Places

As you now know, all things are Brain Matched either consciously or unconsciously. This includes the Brain Matches that we all have of different places.

When I was a child, I used to get an upset stomach almost every time I went to a restaurant. It is not really that I got an upset stomach and felt sick because of the food, but that being in a restaurant just gave me a nervous belly. I would eat fine normally, but it was the restaurant that made me uncomfortable. That continued to happen every time I went to a restaurant as a kid until my Brain Match was changed over time by positive restaurant experiences.

Brain Matches of places are almost always produced by past experiences and the feelings that you've had in that certain place before, and they are almost always unconsciously developed. The reason most people naturally feel comfortable at their house is because their Brain Match with their house is comfort due to the fact that their house is where they have spent some of their most comfortable times, and it is where they sleep almost every night.

Your Brain Matches of places can change when your experiences in that place change. For example, some athletes have tendencies to play better at different stadiums and in different arenas. That is because of their Brain Match with past experiences in that place. If an athlete has a good game in a certain arena, they will tend to have more confidence each time they play there which causes them to play well each time. However, that Brain Match can be altered if that athlete then has a bad performance against a superior team in that same arena.

If you think about it, you will really start to realize that the place you are can affect how you feel and act, and it can also affect your level of confidence. Brain Matches of places is why people think best in certain places and feel more comfortable in different places. Controlling these Brain Matches and recognizing why you have your negative ones is very important. The alteration of a negatively Brain Matched place is the same as altering a Brain Match of a bad experience from the past because those past experiences lead to these Brain Matches of places. If you deliberately change your Brain Match of a past experience at a particular place, then your Brain Match of that place changes in the same respect.

Understanding how Brain Matching works with different places and recognizing why you have certain Brain Matches can help you to overcome mindsets of fear, anxiety, low self-confidence, impatience, and anger. Using the methods to overcome bad experiences can alter these Brain Matches of places for the positive and have you living how you were meant to live, with a positive mindset, regardless of where you are.

Brain Matching People

Do you have those people in your life that no matter what they say or do, they irritate you? Or those people who you always see as awesome and look up to? Two people could tell the exact same joke, and you could laugh at one person and scold the other. Why is that? You guessed it! People, like all other things in life, are Brain Matched.

For example, let's say your annoying co-worker is all over Facebook, posting about their two-week-long vacation that nobody cares about and taking photos of their new cat. When they walk into the office, you cringe with annoyance even if they just get a glass of water and then leave. That's because you've started to associate them with feeling annoyed; therefore, whenever you see that person, you feel annoyed regardless of what they are doing.

How about that singer that you love, you listen to all of their music. You always "like" their Facebook statuses and look at their page often to see pictures of their *incredible* two-week-long vacation and their *adorable* new pet cat! This is simply a Brain Match. You have matched this person with the pleasing feeling that you get when you hear them sing, so every time you see them or something that they are doing, you get that pleasing feeling and have interest even if it is something that you would have no interest in if it was anyone else.

Brain Matching is also how reputations form. Everyone makes a common Brain Match about you due to your actions, so that is how you are then viewed by society. To change your reputation, you simply change your behavior thereby changing peoples' Brain Matches associated with you.

Brain Matching people is not necessarily a bad thing to let happen unconsciously unless you are judging them before you meet them by attaching associations to them according to what they do for work or their family status. Brain Matching people with perfection due to their worldly status is not a good thing to do either. Be conscious of the Brain Matches that you develop and make them for yourself rather than based on the opinions of others.

Using Brain Matches to Alter Habits and Addictions

You can change a negative habit into a positive habit simply by Brain Matching. This form of Brain Matching can help you live the life that you want to live and not be overrun by your negative practices.

Whether it is done consciously or unconsciously, some of us naturally associate foods like this unless it is changed intentionally by you and you only:

Treats and sweets: Yummy
Healthy foods: Boring and not as tasty

Some of us have this Brain Match because we are naturally attracted to the tastiness of the sugar and fat in unhealthy foods as we start to eat them more and more. Over time, we become accustom to eating those sugary, fatty foods—we start to develop the simple habit of unhealthy eating. That is why when you see that box of donuts or that ice cream cake, you naturally want to dig in. It is fine to reward yourself with your favorite treats and snacks, but it is overwhelming when it runs your life and is made into a constant battle every time you enter the kitchen. If you learn to associate unhealthy foods with a bad feeling, such as when you feel sick or guilty from eating them, then you can change your reactions to seeing those foods and therefore reduce the temptation to scarf them down. If you disagree with the Brain Match I just stated, then you have already done this.

If you match up donuts with feeling unhealthy and match up broccoli with making you feel good and nourishing your body, then you will view those foods a lot differently. You might have to close your eyes when you see the donut box with your favorite pastries and envision the guilt of eating one the first couple of times. You are going to have to build up your mental strength, but it will gradually get easier and eventually you will unconsciously walk right past the box of donuts without even noticing it was there. The transformation will look like this:

***Before:* Treats = Yummy Healthy Foods = Boring**
***After:* Treats = Feeling of guilt Healthy Foods = Nourishing**

Some people drag themselves into the gym three days a week. It is all they think about and they dread it all day long. Then, there are other people who love being in the gym and look forward to it all day long. What makes this possible? It is all because of Brain Matching. People who love going to the gym don't necessarily love the pain that running on the treadmill brings; they love the results of that pain. They don't see the weights as *pain*, they see them as *gain*. Some people see weights and think to themselves, *Ugh, look at this weight I have to lift*. Others look at weights and see through the pain of the weight to what the weights will do for them. When those people see weights, they see increased strength.

Weights = Hard work
OR
Weights = Increased strength

Addiction is one of the most influential, life-changing, and life controlling subjects known to mankind. There are "positive" addictions, such as being addicted to exercise, healthy eating, reading, etc. Then, there are those negative addictions. Those are the ones that cause us irritation, can control our lives, and can also control the way we think. Addictions are dangerous because unlike habits, addictions are performed consciously. Repetitive, conscious action can be damaging to your self-esteem and can also harm your relationships. I have life-changing news for you. These vices can most definitely be changed and altered by using Brain Matching.

Unconsciously, Brain Matches are the source of our addictions. In the book, *The Power of Habit,* author Charles Duhigg says that surveys by Alcoholics Anonymous (AA) found that most often peoples' addictions are not driven by intoxication. The researchers concluded that people turn to drugs and alcohol because it offers escape, relaxation, companionship, an opportunity for emotional release, and it helps people to deal with their anxieties.

To simplify this study by AA, every addiction that we have is due to a Brain Match that we have created. For example, why do people smoke? It's because in their brain, they associate smoking with one of those comforting feelings that AA talked about. Every time they feel stress or pressure, they think about smoking because they associate a smoke with comfort.

Smoking = Comfort

The question is then, how can this Brain Match truly be changed, thereby changing an addiction that could even have been life-long up to this point? Firstly, you must identify what it is that your addiction provides you with. You must know *why* you have an addiction in order to change it. Instead of the positive connotation of comfort that is given to smoking, a negative one must be given to it instead. If the thought of smoking's relaxation is changed to how smoking can cause tar to build up in the lungs, then a different association will be given to smoking and it will not be so appealing.

To put conquering an addiction by Brain Matching into a real life setting, let's say you are an inveterate smoker. Instead of thinking about comfort every time you think of smoking, think about more tar building up in your lungs with each cigarette (you can use anything that will help you personally, but this is just an example). Truly close your eyes every time you feel the temptation to pull out the pack and think about the gross tar and gunk that each cigarette contains. Do this until you feel almost uncomfortable that you have smoked before and that you were even just considering smoking. If you do this every single time you think about smoking, it will eventually become a habit for you and it will get easier and easier until you don't even have to think about it. This new perspective will become an unconscious Brain Match, and you will have overcome your addiction.

Smoking = Comfort
DELIBERATELY CHANGED TO
Smoking = Tar buildup in lungs

Brain Matching addictions is very effective and you can Brain Match to whatever severity you need to in order to change. Your Brain Matches that create your habits and addictions can only be changed by making a *deliberate* effort to change them—you must *want* to change. Also, it is *imperative* that you find a healthy alternative solution to provide you with the feeling that you are craving. I cannot stress that enough! If you are craving comfort, you must find a healthy solution that provides the comfort you crave. Whether that solution is talking to family, praying, or yoga, just find something healthy that can replace smoking or whatever your habit or addiction is—something that can provide the comfort that you are looking for. If you don't find an alternative solution, your Brain Match can be changed, but you will then lack something to fill that empty void. That is where other bad habits and addictions can sneak in and you can also fall back more easily into your old addiction because that's all you've ever known to offer you the feeling that you crave.

Most often you can't alter a habit with pure willpower. I heard once that when you operate on willpower, it is like a boat that is being auto-steered south. When you try to turn it around to go north without turning off the auto-steer, you will go a little ways north, but the wheel will always be pulling you back to go south. You will only hang on until your arms get tired, and once you let go, the boat will flip back around and you'll be headed south once more. It is vital to replace your addiction with a healthy solution instead of trying to change through willpower, because if you rely on willpower, you are doomed to fall back into the way you were living before.

You must believe that things can change for you. Don't go into this process expecting failure. Have the faith of a mustard seed and you can move mountains. You most certainly can change these bad habits and unwanted addictions. With God, all things are possible.

Steps in Altering Addictions and Bad Habits

1. Identify your bad habit or addiction
2. Figure out what craving it fulfills

3. Change your Brain Match
4. Find a healthy solution to fill your empty void

Brain Matching a bad habit or addiction will be difficult without plugging in your life to God's Will first. Plugging in your life is not a behavior modification, it's a heart dedication.

Society Impacting Brain Matches

Society can most definitely impact the Brain Matches that you develop and aid in changing them unconsciously over time. This can happen through television, social media, advertisements, your peers, and many other ways.

As The Great Motivator, Les Brown, always says, "Birds of a feather flock together. If you hang out with losers, then you are a loser!" Your closest friends have the biggest impact on who you are as a person.

People always tell me that I am just like my brother. That is because most of my time is spent with him. I have spent more time in my life with him than anyone else. Because of the time we have spent together, we have started to develop the same way of thinking, the same way of talking, and similar ideas. Over the years, my brother and I started to take interest in the same things and began finding similar things humorous.

Knowing and recognizing that you become what you surround yourself with is a huge advantage to becoming the person that you want to be and bettering yourself.

Be deliberate in surrounding yourself with people who are successful and who you look up to. You want to have mentors to teach you many different things and to help make improvements to your mindset. This way you are unconsciously developing similar Brain Matches as them and starting to develop a thought process similar to theirs. You can sometimes achieve the success that you want just by surrounding yourself with the right people and placing yourself in healthy situations.

In a leadership class that I took, my teacher gave us questions to answer for homework. In the homework, one of the questions was, "Who is around your table?" This means, "Who do you surround yourself with?" Imagine a table in your brain where ideas are shared and support is given. Who are the people who you want to have around *your* table when you make decisions each day?

Your Brain Matches can even be influenced by what you watch on television or who you follow on Twitter. If you are constantly looking at the "tweets" of negative people, then you will develop similar thoughts as them. If they associate school to be dreadful, exercise as labor, or work as a requirement rather than an opportunity, then you will unconsciously start to make those associations as well. The more that you are exposed to that kind of pessimistic outlook and the more often you beat those ideas into your head, the stronger those Brain Matches will get.

Television and magazines try to influence us to unconsciously make Brain Matches in our minds as well. A simple example of TV and magazines affecting our Brain

Matches is that society tries to match up doing drugs and being cool as well as sex being a source of fulfillment.

Be aware of your Brain Matches and when they are starting to change. Let them change if you want them to and hold strong in them when you don't. Make sure that you surround yourself with people and situations that let you think freely and develop your own Brain Matches as well as aid you in developing your negative Brain Matches into positive ones.

How Christianity is Brain Matched

Christianity is sometimes strongly Brain Matched by both believers and unbelievers. Sometimes Christians are associated with being crazy or being people who think that everything is an act of God by unbelievers. Unbelievers sometimes think that Christians find no flaws in themselves, and they also see Christianity as a sort of trapped life.

People who are unbelievers sometimes just don't like Christianity because they feel almost guilty inside. That is due to the feeling of God calling them in their lives and them refusing to believe His Word and accept His Grace due to arrogance, and because they Brain Match Christianity with being trapped in a certain way of life and lost pleasure, while believers know that Christianity is actually the opposite.

Even as believers we are sometimes afraid of committing ourselves to God's Will and fully obeying Jesus' teachings because we like our lives how they are and we don't want to give up the things that we love to God. Believers sometimes Brain Match God's Will with risk. They don't fully give their lives up to God so they live half-in and half-out. They come to church, but they don't really pray often or have a relationship with God because they see it as a risky commitment.

One of my cousins runs cross country for his college. One Saturday, he was at a cross country meet and a Christian college there was playing all kinds of music to excite their team before the race. My cousin and another runner were walking by that school's tent and all kinds of Christian music was being played from different artists, such as *TobyMac, Skillet, Relient K,* and a lot of other bands. The other runner with my cousin started to say how he liked the songs. Then, one of his friends came up and told the runner with my cousin that they were Christian songs. After he heard that they were Christian songs, the runner said that the songs actually weren't that good. Had this been his Brain Match with Christianity or Christian music, either way, it was a perfect example of how Brain Matches can influence opinion. Even though he said that he liked the music, his Brain Match immediately made him think differently.

Brain Match Busters

The great speaker and author, Anthony Robbins, once said in response to people who claimed to like surprises, "You like the surprises that you want. The ones you don't want you call 'problems' but you need them." We unconsciously panic when things don't fit with our Brain Matches. That panic can be positive or negative. We have these matches/ associations all set in our brains, and when we set out to do something that we have matched up to give us a good feeling, and we get a bad feeling from it, it messes with our Brain Match, making us furious. This can also be the other way around. We could be doing something that we fear or that we matched up in our heads to give us a bad feeling, and then something could change it and make it a great experience. These experiences are called *Brain Match Busters*. They can be positive or negative, and they can confuse how we feel about our Brain Matches and often change them as well.

God can certainly give us Brain Match Busters and they can also be supplied by other people intentionally. We cannot change a Brain Match that we have developed if we don't deliberately try to change it. Therefore, we cannot give ourselves these busters. They only come from God and other people.

Let's say that you don't like your co-workers. They have always seemed rude, and you just don't get along with them. You don't really like work because of them and you aren't looking forward to going to work on Monday. In fact, let's say it was your birthday on Monday so you are dreading work even more than usual. Then, you show up at work Monday morning and your co-workers have a little surprise birthday party set up for you when you arrive and they all wish you a happy birthday. That surprise would change your

Brain Match regarding your co-workers for sure. That is a positive Brain Match Buster.

Co-workers = Dreadful
BRAIN MATCH BUSTER!!
Co-workers = Caring and thoughtful

An example of a negative Brain Match Buster would be if you look forward to basketball practice after school every single day and you have been starting in every game up to this point. Let's say your Brain Match with basketball is a sense of pride in yourself, but one day, the coach is in a bad mood and yells at you which causes tension between the coach and you, and because of it you don't play much in the next game. That could most definitely change your Brain Match with basketball in a negative way. That is a negative Brain Match Buster.

Basketball = Self-pride
BRAIN MATCH BUSTER!!
Basketball = Tension

Whether you realize it or not, a negative Brain Match Buster is always our cause of anger.

There is a purpose behind all Brain Match Busters, even the negative ones: to steer you in the direction you were meant to go and mold you into the person that you were made to be. These busters are to be thankful for, positive or negative, because they make you into a better version of yourself. Each Brain Match Buster is a wakeup call for growth.

Wrapping Up Brain Matches

Brain Matches are essential to understand, for they are the cause of your thoughts, feelings, likes, dislikes, and they are the controllers of change. Of course, there are many chemicals that are involved in Brain Matching, such as dopamine (the pleasure chemical), but it is really a simple concept to understand and manage.

Understanding and applying the basic methods and principles of Brain Matching will make many of the things that you do in your life more effective, improve your self-discipline, help you to grow into the person that God wants you to be, and also enhance your relationship with Jesus by purifying your life. As you begin to use the concept of Brain Matching, you will be on your way to more easily living a life of fulfillment by plugging in your life.

Life isn't about finding yourself. Life is about creating yourself.
—George Bernard Shaw

4

The Pain Theory

What we see depends mainly on what we look for.
—Sir John Lubbock

I'm sure you've heard the "No pain, no gain" cliché, but the theory that I have discovered called *The Pain Theory* takes it to a further extent. What The Pain Theory simply states is that the only way to grow is by going through some sort of pain. Also, the more intense the pain is, the more dramatic the growth is. Whether that pain is mental, spiritual, or physical, it has to be encountered in order to grow. Although the only way to cultivate growth is through pain, not all pain causes growth. For example, a broken arm does not end up in growth. Everything in life is proved by this theory. It is simply a law of the universe.

The Pain Theory:
Growth REQUIRES Pain
Pain DOESN'T ALWAYS MEAN Growth

As you know from Anthony Robbins, growth is needed in order to experience fulfillment in life. Therefore, according to my theory, we must encounter pain in order to experience fulfillment.

Pain = Growth = Fulfillment
THEREFORE
Pain = Fulfillment

Eliminating Fear of Pain

If you look hard enough for something, you're eventually going to find what you are looking for. If you looked hard enough, you could find flaws with every single person in the world. They could be the nicest, most attractive person you have ever seen, but if you look hard enough, you could find that they have odd earlobes. That is an outlandish example, but you get the point (yes, go in the mirror and take a look—you know you want to).

Pain is something that most people are afraid of. I'm not talking about the broken arm, physically hurt kind of pain. I'm talking about the strenuous pain, the pain that challenges us and pushes us beyond our comfort zone. Some people tend to search unconsciously through each area of their life to look for pain. Eventually, pain becomes evident to them and the negative side of the things they focus on starts to show. An example of this is working out. Some people unconsciously use most of their energy to focus on the pain that it brings instead of searching for the positive effects it will have on them.

Boredom comes from a lack of growth. When someone doesn't see improvement toward achieving their goals, growth in their relationships, or improvement any area of their life really, this lack of growth causes people to become bored with what they are doing. A common way that people try to solve this boredom is by changing the things that they don't see growth in. If they don't see growth with one goal, they will change their goals. If their relationship is not growing, they get bored and change their relationship. It is a simple cycle of life. We actually crave the growth that pain brings us. That being said, in a way, we all crave pain.

Whether you admit it or not, you don't like change. Nobody likes change because it is uncomfortable; however, we all crave the growth that comes from it. We crave the change that we don't like. How does that work?

For example, when someone's dog dies, why are they compelled to buy a new dog? It is because they need to fill that void that they now have from losing their dog, so they go to the store and pick out a new dog, usually similar to the one they had before. Not many people will buy a pit-bull after their poodle dies. They will buy another poodle or a dog similar to their previous one. That is because the poodle is comfortable and familiar to them. After they buy the dog, they are content once again and their void of losing their old dog is fulfilled through this change of buying the similar new dog.

When people are bored with their relationship because it isn't growing the way they want it to, they break up with the other person. That is a painful process; however, it leads to growth in the end because of the mental strength needed to get through the break up and the knowledge that comes from it. Then, the people in that relationship will search for similar people to fill the void of that loss. The reason that people get back together after a break up sometimes is because they love the comfort but crave growth in the change of the break up itself.

God designed us to crave growth that comes from change but dislike change. He gives us enough change to grow but enough similarities to keep us comfortable and secure. That is why He designed different seasons so that we could have the change we desire, but the fact that we know when the seasons are coming and can predict their order keeps us secure and comfortable.

Some pain is pain that we don't choose to experience. This kind of pain could come from the death of a pet or a crushed relationship. It's not always the news that we want to hear, but these events really do make us stronger and result in growth. We learn to cope with these different events and improve because of them. Out of these tough times, we develop stronger relationships and find things out about ourselves that we didn't know before. There is a positive way to look at everything. Your choice is just whether you chose to accept that fact or not.

You can grow or be comfortable, but you can't do both at the same time.
—*Unknown truth*

Embrace Pain

We must embrace pain and burn it as fuel for our journey.
—*Kenji Miyazawa*

If the only way to grow is through pain, then why do most people fear pain? It's not that we fear growth, but we fear the change that causes the growth. We fear that change because it is uncomfortable—change is often painful.

Sometimes we become so comfortable with our lifestyle and our level of pain that we go through daily that we don't want anything to change us and throw things off course. In one way or another, we all strive to be comfortable. In reality, nobody wants to be uncomfortable. We will complain about bad things in our life, but we won't make an effort to change those things because we don't want to take a chance that the good things will change as well. That causes us to become stuck in a tough situation.

The right thing to do in this situation is to focus on the areas that you want to grow in. When you focus on these areas, you will experience pain to make you better in those areas, but that will be ok because you really want that change. You must want change because you are focused on the benefits of your pain. You know you have the right mentality when you say "Bring on the pain, because I want the growth!"

Sometimes we get upset with God because He is letting us experience great pain, but God lets us go through pain sometimes to help us grow in a way that we wouldn't grow without Him letting us experience and work through that pain. Kyle Idleman explains in his book, *AHA*, that the number-one contributor to spiritual growth is *difficult circumstances.*

The Ultimate Pain

So will it be with the resurrection of the dead. The body that is sown is perishable, it is raised imperishable; it is sown in dishonor, it is raised in glory; it is sown in weakness, it is raised in power; it is sown a natural body, it is raised a spiritual body. If there is a natural body, there is also a spiritual body.
—1 Corinthians 15:42-44 NIV

The Pain Theory states that more pain creates more growth. For example, if you exercise more, thereby putting yourself through more pain, you will have more growth in that area than if you exercise less. Those who study more, thereby putting themselves through more mental pain, will acquire more knowledge than those who study less. Your growth is a reflection of the pain that you are put through in that particular area.

The Pain Theory solves one of the ultimate human fears: death. When we experience the ultimate pain of death, our life taken away from us, we reap the ultimate reward: eternal life in Heaven. God, in His infinite Wisdom, created this special law of your pain reflecting your growth. That is the nature of all things. This life contains pain, but the ultimate growth—your home in Heaven—is free if it, so keep your mind focused on the growth ahead, and fix your eyes on Jesus, the only way home.

He will wipe away every tear from their eyes, and death shall be no more, neither shall there be mourning, nor crying, nor pain anymore, for the former things have passed away.
—Revelation 21:4 ESV

Brain Matching The Pain Theory

Pain births growth. That is a simple Brain Match that should be developed within your mind. I talked about this particular Brain Match briefly in the last chapter, but I would like to expand on it in this section.

What you focus on is what you will see. That focus will then consume what you do. That can work for you in a positive way, but also in a negative way. Choose to focus on growth instead of pain, because pain will only bring growth. Be thankful for the pain you experience, because the more pain that you are put through, either by choice or by God, is helping you to grow so that you will become a better version of yourself.

People tend to associate pain with the feeling it initially gives them. This feeling is uncomfortable and not something that anyone would particularly choose to experience. Pain may be uncomfortable, but motivational speaker Eric Thomas has a famous quote that I really like and it set in with me deeply when I heard it. He says, "Become comfortable with being uncomfortable." Simply find comfort in the pain that you experience. Nobody would choose to put themselves through pain if they didn't reap some sort of reward from it, and God wouldn't put you through anything if good didn't come out of it.

You might be at the breaking point where you feel like you can't take any more pain, but really, you are just a slingshot. The more you get stretched, the further God will propel you at His divine time. Each day that your faith gets stretched, remember that God is taking you that much further when the right time comes. Choose to focus on that reward rather than the pain itself. All pains are growing pains. Change your Brain Match.

Pain = Uncomfortable feeling
DELIBERATELY CHANGED TO
Pain = Growth

My dad runs a very steep hill a couple times almost every night. He is getting in better shape and becoming healthier because of it. Every time I've run the hill with him, he seems to be in a lot of pain and is always out of breath. That doesn't sound like something that is particularly fun to me, but he truly loves running the hill. Why would he love running a hill that puts him through so much pain? It's because he doesn't see the hill as pain. Instead, he associates the hill with his health. Every time he thinks of the hill, consciously or unconsciously, he thinks about his health. If he were to focus on the pain of the hill, he would not be as enthused to run it, and he would not put as much energy and effort into it. That would cause a decrease in productivity and change his Brain Match that he has created of the hill and also of his health. Instead of living joyfully, he would live in anxiety of the hill, because he would be thinking about the pain all day long, and a healthy lifestyle would seem more difficult to him.

Hill = Pain

OR

Hill = Improved health and better shape

There are many ways to grow your mind, but physical endurance is the best way to grow mentally. The ability to endure is not just a physical battle, but a matter of how much you are willing to stretch your mental growth.

Growing to New Levels

Growth is essential to living a fulfilling life, and it only develops through pain. Pain is positive, not negative. Without it, life would lack fulfillment. God has put pain on this earth so that we could grow and expand our faith in Him.

Don't see the pain. See through that to the growth. What you focus on, you will get. When you focus on your growth and enjoy what you do, your action is no longer difficult—it's inspired action. When you start focusing on the growth that your pain will bring, you aren't trying to force something to happen; instead, things just begin to happen for you.

5

An Attitude of Gratitude

Develop an attitude of gratitude, and give thanks for everything that happens to you, knowing that every step forward is a step toward achieving something bigger and better than your current situation.
—Brian Tracy

Developing an attitude of gratitude is done by making a habit out of recognizing the things and people in your life that you are thankful for and loving them.

Every single morning, as you get ready for your upcoming day, think about all of the things in your life that you are grateful for. By doing this, you are setting yourself up for a day filled with even more things to be grateful for. Make it a priority to notice all of the things in your life that bring you joy throughout the day. At the end of each day, take a couple of minutes to reflect on how your day went. As you begin to live gratefully, you will start to notice good things and positive people in your life that you haven't noticed before because you haven't taken the time to really pay attention to them.

I like what Kyle Idleman says in his book, *Gods at War*. He explains, "God has given us the use of his resources for a short time here on earth, and we have much to be grateful for. Go through your day sometime just recognizing that everything is God's. Get out of God's bed and walk into God's bathroom, and turn on God's shower, and then put on God's clothes. Eat God's cereal and drink God's coffee. Get in God's car and head to work. When we start to see all of our resources as God's it helps us develop an attitude of gratitude that leads to a heart of worship."

For we brought nothing into the world, and
we can take nothing out of it.
—1 Timothy 6:7 NIV

Everything belongs to God, so live each day with that understanding prominently in your mind.

Bold, Grateful Prayer

I was in church one Sunday when I was really young and the pastor told a story of a man who was a very faithful Christian. A lady once asked him what he prayed about and what he asked God for. He replied by saying that he doesn't ask God for anything. The only thing that he did when he prayed was thank God for all the things and people He had provided him with and all that He had done for him and his family. He said that God had given him so much, so why would he constantly beg for more?

The pastor's words have been ingrained in my head and have altered the way that I have prayed ever since. Most of us beg for things from God, and we are irritated if He doesn't provide them for us the way we want, but if we actually take time to notice and be grateful for all that He does for us in our lives and for His children, then our faith and the way we pray will be forever changed.

Before you ask God for something that you want, think about all that He has provided for you already and make sure to take some time to be grateful for the work that He does. Thanking God for what He does for you regularly will change the way you think about your life and the way God works.

Don't let me fool you into thinking that God doesn't want you to ask Him for things because He loves giving gifts to His children. I like what Paul says in Romans 8:32 when he states, *"He who did not spare his own Son, but gave Him up for us all—how will He not also, along with Him, graciously give us all things?" (NIV)*

Joel Osteen is the Pastor of Lakewood Church in Houston, Texas. In one of his sermons online, he says that God delights in bold prayers. He wants you to show your faith in Him through your bold belief. Pastor Osteen says often, "We are victors, not victims." We are victorious through our faith. We are by no means a victim of anything. We know this because God is for us.

If God is for us, who can be against us?
—Romans 8:31 NIV

Bold is defined by Dictionary.com as, "not hesitating or fearful in the face of actual or possible danger or rebuff; courageous and daring." God wants us to pray prayers that are daring and courageous, that demonstrate our strong belief in what is possible with Him on our side.

God sees things from a drastically different perspective than we do. He understands our perspective, but He can see it all. Some people, for example, pray to God to help them get out of debt; however, God's Power is mighty. You must understand that He can do *anything*. He has infinite Power. Instead of praying for God to help you get out of debt, a bold prayer would be to pray for abundant cash to provide your family with all that they need and more.

God doesn't see audacious prayers as demanding. Instead, He sees them as your strong faith in His Power. God delights in bold prayer.

> *This is the confidence we have in approaching God: that if we ask anything according to His Will, He hears us. And if we know that He hears us—whatever we ask—we know that we have what we asked of Him.*
> *—1 John 5:14-17 NIV*

To take this a step further, there is a way to show your gratefulness by praying boldly as well. Thank God ahead of time for what you have faith in Him to give you. That demonstrates strong belief in God's ability and will expand your own faith.

An example of thanking God ahead of time through bold prayer would be if you are praying about your mother's health. If you were praying about that, you might pray a prayer similar to, "Please help restore my mother's health and guide us all through this time." That prayer is fine, but to expand your belief in the prayer, you could alter that prayer into, "Thank you for the restoration that You are bringing to my mother, and thank You that You are guiding us all through this time."

Therefore I tell you, whatever you ask for in prayer,
believe that you have received it, and it will be yours.
—Mark 11:24 NIV

By no means is this a staple that you must pray by. God sees prayers from the heart, not how we word them. Some people get worried about not praying correctly or not using the elaborate words that a pastor might use. That does not change how faithful you are by any means, and God does not view prayer by your standard of grammar or fluctuation of vocabulary. God simply sees your prayers through your heart and through your passion for what you are praying about. However, praying bold and grateful prayers will aggrandize *your own* faith. Praying bold prayers will help you to believe more in what you are saying to God and aid you in coming to the reality that what you are praying for can and will be taken care of by God.

The LORD does not look at the things people look at. People look at the outward appearance, but the LORD looks at the heart.
—1 Samuel 16:7 NIV

In the midst of hardships, in the event of a calamity, do you pray for a way *out* or a way *through*? Bold prayers expand your faith most during difficult times. Plugging in your life means to have faith in God that what He is testing you with will make you stronger. God doesn't let anything happen without His permission.

Keeping track of what you pray about in a prayer journal will really help you to better yourself and will help strengthen your relationship with God. A strong, personal, and growing relationship with God will most definitely lead to a life of fulfillment.

Many people will say that they pray, but God just brings them more struggle and dissatisfaction. They wonder why God won't answer their prayers. In the movie *Evan Almighty*, Morgan Freeman (who plays God) says, "If someone prays for patience, do you think God gives them patience? Or does he give them the opportunity to be patient? If they pray for courage, does God give them courage, or does he give them opportunities to be courageous? If someone prayed for their family to be closer, you think God zaps them with warm, fuzzy feelings? Or does he give them opportunities to love each other?"

Sometimes when you think God isn't answering prayer the way that you want, and that He is just making things more difficult, He's actually blessing you with opportunities to grow. You just have to learn how to notice those opportunities and keep your mind open to the signs that God sends you.

Feel Grateful

Living with an attitude of gratitude is deeper than just noticing good things that are in your life and identifying things that you are thankful for. To live gratefully, you must *feel* grateful. You have to develop a passion for being grateful and allow the things that you are grateful for to really resonate in your heart.

By feeling grateful, you will begin to be happy for what you have and you will start developing into more of an optimist rather than having a pessimistic point of view. When you are grateful for the little things in your life, and when you develop a positive, grateful attitude, it becomes a habit to be grateful for everything—even the "negative."

Living with an attitude of gratitude and noticing things that you are thankful for will also boost your self-confidence. You will begin to notice your strengths more than your weaknesses and notice more of your better qualities rather than your weaker ones.

Joel Osteen told a story one Sunday at Lakewood Church that was about these kids who played a prank on their grandfather while he was sleeping. The children got some old cheese and put it all over his mustache. Eventually, their grandfather started to become uncomfortable and he began to wake up. When he woke up, he sniffed and proclaimed, "It stinks in here." He then went into the kitchen to get out of the stink. He sniffed again, expecting a better smell, and said that the whole house stinks. He went outside to get some fresh air and took a big deep breath, but again smelled the rotten cheese smell. He proclaimed, "The whole world stinks."

At times we think that things on the outside are amiss and we feel sorry for ourselves. We believe that problems are going on all around us and that we are put in all of these complicated situations, but the reality is you need to evaluate *yourself* in these situations. Look at yourself before you look at outer sources, because your mindset, positive or negative, branches into every aspect of your life. Don't walk around with rotten cheese on your mustache. Wipe it off and smell the fresh air.

First take the plank out of your own eye, and then you will see clearly to remove the speck from your brother's eye.
—Matthew 7:5 NIV

Once you develop a habit recognizing things that you are grateful for, the negative things in your life will seem small compared to all of the positive things that you are grateful for.

You can't live a positive life thinking negative thoughts.
—Joel Osteen

Altering Your Mindset

Even if life is wearing you down, learn to be grateful in the little things. Be grateful that your car is running and that you can get yourself to work. Be grateful that your family is healthy. Be grateful that you have a talent or a special ability. Be grateful that God is always with you. Be grateful that it is a sunny day. Just be grateful for every single thing in your life, and over time it will become a habit. You will be surprised at how much just having a grateful mindset can impact your life and how much joy it will bring you.

As I was researching for a story about living life gratefully, I stumbled upon a post by Kabir Mahadeva on *activerain.trulia.com.* The post was entitled, *A Parable About Being Thankful.* The story really hit on many key points about changing your current mindset into a grateful mindset.

A blind boy sat on the steps of a building with a hat by his feet. He held up a sign which said: "I am blind, please help." There were only a few coins in the hat.

A man was walking by. He took a few coins from his pocket and dropped them into the hat. He then took the sign, turned it around, and wrote some words. He put the sign back so that everyone who walked by would see the new words. Soon the hat began to fill up.

A lot more people were giving money to the blind boy. That afternoon the man who had changed the sign came to see how things were. The boy recognized his footsteps and asked,

"Were you the one who changed my sign this morning? What did you write?"

The man said, "I only wrote the truth. I said what you said but in a different way." I wrote: "Today is a beautiful day but I cannot see it."

Both signs told people that the boy was blind. But the first sign simply said the boy was blind. The second sign told people that they were so lucky that they were not blind. Should we be surprised that the second sign was more effective?

This parable is a great example of the mindset change that has to occur in order to live with a grateful mindset. Instead of focusing on being blind, the negative, the focus was switched to being grateful for the beautiful day. That switch from a pessimistic point of view to an optimistic point of view changed the way people reacted to the blind boy and the Brain Matches that they made with him. Instead of being a begging blind boy on the side of the road, he turned into a grateful boy with an unfortunate circumstance that people were willing to help.

When things in your life fall apart, when everything seems to go wrong, what will you choose to focus on? What will your mindset be? Will you have thoughts that are positive or negative? These moments are a test of your gratitude. They are a test of your faith. Choose to be grateful for the things that you still have in the disagreeable times. You will always have things to be grateful for, no matter what. All you have to do is take the time to notice and appreciate them.

"Grate" Success

Applying these methods to your life and altering your current mindset to a more grateful mindset will propel you further as you strive for your goals and dreams.

Your goals will seem within your grasp by living with an attitude of gratitude, because they are. God will provide you with all you need in order to make the impossible possible for you. You were born to fulfill God's purpose for your life, so He will provide you with all of the necessary abilities and give you the obstacles that are required in order to create the best version of yourself that can handle His favor in your future. Trust in the Lord to steer you down the right path and be grateful for all of the struggles, because it is in the struggle that He molds us most.

Yet You, LORD, are our Father. We are the clay, You are the potter; we are all the work of Your hand.
—Isaiah 64:8 NIV

Grateful for Fulfillment

Developing an attitude of gratitude is a life-changing switch. This switch will alter the way people view you, the way you handle different situations and problems, your level of joy, and the way you view yourself and your life.

Every time you do anything, be grateful for the opportunity to do it. *Everything* is an opportunity, and *nothing* is an obligation. Live with that simple truth in your mind each day.

Rejoice always, pray continually, give thanks in all circumstances; for this is God's Will for you in Christ Jesus.
—1 Thessalonians 5:16-18 NIV

6

Goals

Do not offer any part of yourself to sin as an instrument of wickedness, but rather offer yourselves to God as those who have been brought from death to life; and offer every part of yourself to Him as an instrument of righteousness.
—Romans 6:13 NIV

God has given you special gifts to fulfill a divine purpose here on earth. He wants you to offer yourself as an instrument of righteousness. You are a specially created instrument, but only God knows how to play you the right way. Plugging in your life means to let God make beautiful music with your life. Plugging in your life is a spiritual sacrifice to give your life up to God and a physical commitment to fulfill His plan for your life by chasing after your divine goals and dreams. God's Will is the outlet, and your goals and dreams are the cord.

What runs this world, accomplishes great things, and develops everyone's daily routine, is goals. Goals make the world grow and keep dreams alive. If you aren't striving for anything, then you aren't growing, and you are missing a huge chunk of fulfillment in life.

Life is naturally up and down. My eighth grade English teacher once said to me, "Life has ups and downs. If you don't have ups and downs in your life, then you are flat-lined—your life is dead." If you let life control who you are and what you do, you will end up living like everyone else. You will have ups and downs, and things will happen *to you*. Plugging in your life means to not let things happen *to you* in life, but to instead go out and happen *to things*. Average people will always live with the feeling that they are capable of more, but they will never go out and achieve more. Don't live another average day in your life, because God created you to be everything but average.

You were made specifically to have God's light shine through you in all areas of your life. The ultimate goal each day is to do things that please God and make Him smile. Choose to praise Him by doing the things that you love and by striving for the goals and dreams that He has placed in your heart.

Process of Setting Goals

Set the kind of goals that will make something of you to achieve them. What I mean by that is to set goals that will change who you are and make you a better version of yourself. We all crave change and we all desire growth. Growth is the nature of all things and without it, you die internally. You want goals that will put you through struggle, challenge you, change how you think, and mold you into the best version of yourself. If you are capable of achieving your goals without changing who you are, then your goals aren't big enough. It is necessary to set goals that you have to grow into and that require a change that will make you into a greater version of yourself.

Dreams come a size too big so we can grow into them.
—Josie Bisset

You must set both short and long-term goals. Short-term goals will give you something to work towards on your way to your long-term goals. Short-term goals could be within a week, a month, three months, or even a year or two. Long-term goals are those things that you aspire to do or be one day that will take time and require a change in who you are.

It is essential to have short-term goals because without them, everything would seem so distant and you would be more likely to give up. That is why when most young people set out to be professional athletes, they work hard for a couple of months, but then that work ethic starts to fade. It fades because the dream seems to be so far away. Sometimes certain people still persevere through that concept; however, that is not very often at all. Almost all professional athletes and successful people who you know today have set short-term goal after short-term goal to eventually get to where they are today.

Long-term goals are needed because without them, you would not have a big picture. Long-term goals give you a target for your passions and they provide you with direction for where you want to go in your life. Knowing your long-term goals and being committed to achieving them will simplify decision-making in your life. When you are committed to achieving your specific goals, they will start making decisions *for* you.

For example, if you are debating whether you should go out late at night to a party, ask your goals. If you are in the kitchen and aren't sure what to eat, ask your goals. Your goals may allow you to go out to a party every weekend or eat unhealthy foods, but if your goal is to lose 50 pounds, when you go into the kitchen and don't know whether to eat salad or pasta, ask your goal. Your goal will tell you to choose salad. Before you take any action, ask yourself if it is helping or hindering your goals.

Another type of goal that is good to set is a daily goal. Don't get this confused with a to-do list (which I will get to later). Make your daily goal one specific thing that you would like to accomplish that day. It can be the same each day or it can vary. It all depends on your schedule and what you want to do with your day. Ask yourself, "What one thing will give me success today?" When you focus on that one daily goal, everything that you do in the day will revolve around achieving that goal. This will make for more and more positive, progressive, and successful days.

A prerequisite when setting every goal is to ask yourself, "Does my goal honor God?" and, "Is this goal just for my own satisfaction, or is it to bring glory to God?" If your goals are just for personal satisfaction or for attention, then your goals are not really worth pursuing and your successes are futile in the long run. Reevaluate your goals. Think about if what you are doing actually matters when it's all said and done. When you die, will your goals and dreams matter?

Unless the LORD builds a house, the
work of the builders is wasted.
—Psalm 127:1 NLT

It is vital to set tangible goals. You will burn out if you set goals that are vague. For example, let's say you bench press 225 pounds and you want to bench more weight. Your goal can't be to "bench more weight" because there is no way of determining your success. A good goal would be to say that you want to bench 245 pounds. That way you can determine when you achieve your goal.

Also, putting a time frame on your goals can be helpful especially with short-term goals. Using the same example, you could say that you want to increase your bench to 245 pounds by a certain date. That is a specific, tangible goal and the time will also hold you accountable to work for it by sticking to a plan and not procrastinating. Putting a time frame on your goals eliminates the, "One day I'll do it" phrase.

Setting goals that stretch you is needed in order to find true joy in what you are aspiring to do. You need to have goals that will require you to operate on the next level, physically and mentally.

Sometimes you might doubt that you are capable of achieving a certain goal that you are striving for or doubt that you can get past a failure. However, doubts arise when we neglect to look at God. When you realize how big and powerful your God is, there is no room for doubt. When you realize and understand that God is in control and can do absolutely anything, then doubt just seems petty. Doubt cannot exist when the Power of God is kept in perspective. As you let God work through you, all things are possible for your life.

The greatest danger for most of us is not that our aim is too high and we miss, but that our aim is too low and we hit.
—Michelangelo

Failure and Hardship

But He said to me, "My Grace is sufficient for you, for My Power is made perfect in weakness." Therefore I will boast all the more gladly of my weaknesses, so that the Power of Christ may rest upon me. For the sake of Christ, then, I am content with weaknesses, insults, hardships, persecutions, and calamities. For when I am weak, then I am strong.
—2 Corinthians 12:9-12 ESV

In the hard times of life, when you fail, when you get knocked down, when you feel weak, where do you turn?

God's Power is perfected in our weakness. We all have weaknesses and we all fail at some point in life at something. It is in these hard times and in these weaknesses that God's Power shines brightest in our lives.

And we know that in all things God works for the good of those who love Him, who have been called according to His purpose.
—Romans 8:28 NIV

God will use the failures in your life to ultimately promote you towards your goals and dreams that He has put in you. As I have stated in the "Attitude of Gratitude" chapter, you must be thankful for the hard times because it is through these difficulties that God molds you most. God isn't interested in changing your circumstances, He is interested in changing *you*.

You do not realize now what I am doing,
but later you will understand.
—John 13:7 NIV

Up to a month before I began writing this book, I was never sure what I wanted to do with my life. All I really cared about was setting goals for sports and achieving those goals. My goals were things like winning a state championship, gaining all-state honors, playing Division 1 college sports, and being a professional athlete.

In the span of about a month, everything changed and who I am now was developed; however, my life was not developed in a way that I would have chosen. In my sophomore football season, after a great start to the year, I had to leave the game just before half time. I was starting varsity on both sides of the ball against a rival team, and I began struggling from exhaustion and shortness of breath as the game went on. I didn't think that it was anything serious. I thought that I was just exhausted and really run down. The team doctors checked me out, and my mom thought that it was anxiety because I had been struggling badly with it the week preceding the game. I would wake up in the middle of the night with chills and in a panic. I'd have to calm down, sometimes for hours, before returning to bed. I was going through a really hard time, and I didn't understand why.

The week after the game, I started to notice swollen glands and soreness throughout my body. I went to the doctor, and he thought that I might have strep throat; however, that was not the case. After having my blood drawn (I don't like needles), I tested positive for mononucleosis (mono).

Finding out that I had mono was a huge blow to me. It took me out of all physical activity for six weeks along with having to come back with a plodding recovery, pretty much putting a close to my football season, creeping into my basketball season, and also limiting me from going to school full days.

You might be able to imagine how that would feel to be so excited about something, setting goals for it, having it be your focus, and then having it taken away from you. That was a hard time for me, and I felt weak physically, mentally, and spiritually without anything to feed my passion for sports that I have had my whole life. Little did I know at the time, but this perceived curse was a blessing in disguise from God.

Before being diagnosed with mono, I used to listen to motivational and inspirational tapes and podcasts while I trained for sports, such as speeches by Eric Thomas, Anthony Robbins, Jim Rohn, Joel Osteen, Les Brown, Earl Nightingale, and many more. Up until my sickness, I also enjoyed reading, but I never really had the time to pick up a book. I have always been interested in motivational quotes, speeches, and loved learning about life and following dreams. However, aside from my tapes and videos, I would only read about one book every six months.

Because of mono holding me back from participating in physical activities, I made a habit of reading first thing in the morning when I turned off my alarm. I began to read the books that I had on my shelf that I intended on reading "eventually." My initial mono lasted five long weeks—not counting working back to my normal which took a couple of extra weeks. In that five week span, I read four books. This little change of habit changed the way I lived my life. I began loving books and wanting to read and expand my knowledge to the point where I would rather read than watch an entertaining TV show.

Cast all your anxiety on Him because He cares for you.
—1 Peter 5:7 NIV

God wants to hear what worries you, and He wants you to be real with Him. He will listen when nobody else will and care more than anyone else ever could. Because of the anxiety that came with my mono, I began to cast my anxiety on God instead of trying to deal with it on my own. I would pray to God and tell Him everything that was worrying me or stressing me out. By doing that, it enhanced my relationship with Him and changed everything. It became a commitment for me to go to church every Sunday rather than an option. I now *want* to be there more than anywhere else. I love the presence that the church brings: worshiping and learning about God while surrounded by other Christians doing the same. It's truly wonderful.

Because of mono, my mindset and motivation was no longer *me*-based, it became *God*-based. I didn't know that I was headed in a direction I wasn't meant to go in, but through that turnaround and hard time in my life, God molded me into the person that I was meant to be and has steered me in a direction of true purpose and fulfillment in my life. I always had something missing in my life, something holding me back from true joy, but because of what looked like a "hardship" in my life, I am now living fulfilled. Dealing with a hardship is sometimes the boost that you need in order to get over the hills of life. God sometimes lets our lives fall apart so that we turn to Him to build them back up His way. Sometimes God can't be everything to you until He's the only thing you have left.

One day you will be able to look back at the failures and hard times in your life and see them as stepping stones to your current successes.

You will fail your way to success.
—Les Brown

Failure is bound to happen when you strive to achieve a goal or a dream. It is inevitable. The question, however, is how do you deal with that failure?

Failure is growth in disguise. The more we fail, the stronger we become because of the pain that we endure and learn from. If you focus on your failures and not your successes, your successes will become less evident, and you will begin to lose confidence in yourself and your dreams, because you won't recognize the progress that you are making due to being caught up in your failures. In short, your energy goes where your focus lies.

Every time you fail, don't focus on the failure itself; instead, focus on what caused you to fail and work to ameliorate or improve those areas of your life. When you learn from your failures, you will become stronger with each failure and eventually develop into a version of yourself that can achieve the success that you are striving for.

Sometimes in life we have what seem like repetitive, constant failures. You will keep failing at the same thing if you don't learn why you failed. For example, if I want to make cupcakes and don't use baking powder, my cupcakes will always turn out flat no matter how many times I try.

I will continue to fail until I figure out the reason for my failure and learn from it. That is how I can learn from failure to make delicious cupcakes and thereby help others to do the same. Embrace your failures instead of dwelling over them. With each failure, you are one step closer to your dreams.

The fear of failure can cause you to lose track of your dreams, live with unfulfilled potential, and prohibit you from living out your purpose in life. The fear of failure can be a trap that keeps you from fulfillment, but the freedom to fail often results in greater accomplishments. Failure just means that the certain path you are on isn't the way that you were meant to achieve that goal. In Romans 5:3-4, Paul says, *"...suffering produces perseverance; perseverance, character; and character, hope." (NIV)* Some translations replace the word "perseverance" with "patience," and the word "suffering" with "endurance." Suffering requires perseverance, but enduring requires patience. It takes patience to persevere, and that patience is fed by faith. Your success will reflect your ability to persevere—your patience. Your failures are not the defining moments of your life or career, but your responses to them can be.

Fear is a self-imposed prison that will keep you from becoming what God intended for you to be.
—Rick Warren

In your hands, you hold the key to your success. All you have to do is find the right door, the door which your key unlocks. You may see ten other people unlock the same door to a dream similar to yours, but your key doesn't unlock that door. That doesn't mean that you can't have your dream. You just have to find your own door, your own way. Every time you fail, think to yourself, *This just isn't my door, but I will never stop looking, because I have the key to my success.*

So do not fear, for I am with you; do not be dismayed,
for I am your God. I will strengthen you and help you;
I will uphold you with My righteous right hand.
—Isaiah 41:10 NIV

Vision

The only thing worse than being blind
is having sight but no vision.
—Helen Keller

Writing things down is powerful in that you can visually see it for yourself. Writing down your goals and reading over them often makes them clearer in your head. My Bible teacher at my school makes every one of his students memorize a long Bible verse each quarter of the school year. Before each test, he makes everyone write the whole verse out three times. Why would he do that? It is because writing something out triggers muscle memory, and it also helps his students to see and better master the verse. My teacher said that before he made his students write the verse out three times, three fourths of his students would fail the test, and the verse was a fourth of the length that it is now. Now that he makes his students write the verse out three times, over half of his students get a perfect score on every test!

Another way to make your goals visual along with writing them down is to create a vision board. That is most often a collage of pictures of things that you hope to have, places you want to go, and things that you want to accomplish. You put this collage up in a place that you will see it often, and it gives you a visual of what you want. Sometimes we have these big goals that seem so difficult to achieve, but if you have a visual picture of what you want, it will help you to develop more focused goals in your mind.

Visualizing is monumental in achieving goals, big or small. It can even influence whether you have a good or bad day. Personally, I use visualization for almost everything I do. This is the art of closing your eyes and playing out situations in your mind the way you want them to go, then thinking about any difficulties that you might encounter and how you would overcome them. Finally, when you open up your eyes, all you have to do is live out your vision.

For example, before a test, I close my eyes, picture myself having the test in front of me, taking the test, writing down the answers, feeling good about it, and getting a great grade. When I open my eyes, I have already gotten a great grade on my test, so all I have to do then is take it.

In the morning, schedule some time for visualization. Think about your schedule for the day. Close your eyes and visualize going through that schedule in as much detail as you need to in order to provide a clear picture of what your day will look like. Visualize the best case scenario and then think about any problems that you might encounter and how you will solve those and still maintain a confident outlook. Visualize a superb day. After that, open your eyes and live it out.

Visualizing your goals works the same way as visualizing anything else. Close your eyes and create a vision for what you want. Make your vision very precise and detailed. Visualize yourself achieving the goal that you are committed to achieving. Really feel what it will feel like to achieve that goal. Then, open your eyes and realize that the goal that you are striving for has already been achieved. After that, all you have to do is go get it. Act as if your name is on your goal, because it is.

Writing your goals down and having a visual of what you want will help you to see your goals more clearly in your mind and organize your thoughts. That way you can manage your goals better and create a more effective plan to achieve them.

Decide what you want. Believe you can have it. Believe you deserve it and believe it's possible for you. And then close your eyes every day for several minutes, and visualize having what you already want, feeling the feelings of already having it. Come out of that and focus on what you're grateful for already, and really enjoy it. Then go into your day and release it to the Universe and trust that the Universe will figure out how to manifest it.
—*Jack Canfield*

Plan of Action

If you wait for perfect conditions, you will never get anything done.
—Ecclesiastes 11:4 NIV

If you are waiting for the right time to start working toward your dream, it's not going to happen. As it is with deciding to follow Jesus, there will never be a perfect time to start working towards your goals and dreams; you must *create* the perfect time to start—and that time is right now. Your life is like an early morning, and the more you press the snooze button, the easier it gets and the more you lose. Right now, you have to make the decision to begin the journey to achieving your dreams. Don't waste another moment of your precious life by procrastinating and making excuses.

So many people wait till January 1st, wait till next month, wait till they get out of debt, and make all of these excuses why they can't start now. Do not *talk* about getting started and achieving your goals, go out and get them. You can say it one time and write it down, but then you must get to work. Don't go around telling everyone about your goals and dreams, but then not take any action to achieve them because you need approval from everyone first. You have God's approval, and you must give yourself your own. Those are the only two opinions that matter when you decide to start moving towards your goals and dreams. It is time to take action toward what you want to achieve and worship God by doing it.

If you try to catch two rabbits, you will not catch either one.
—Russian Proverb

You cannot run after so many different things and try to change your focus on and off of your different goals. That does not mean you can't have more than one goal at a time, but the goals that you have should be somewhat in line with each other in order to achieve them. Most of the time it takes all of your focus to achieve a big dream. If it doesn't, then you are capable of more than what you are striving for.

An intelligent person aims at wise action, but
a fool starts off in many directions.
—Proverbs 17:24 GNT

Plugging in your life means choosing to develop into a person that can achieve the goals you long for. The person that you are when you start off on your journey is not the person that you are when you achieve your goals. The path toward your goals and dreams will develop the best version of you. What you do each day develops who you are, so the bigger the goals that you set, the bigger the progress you will make as an individual.

Implement into your day one thing, big or small, that will help you to achieve your goal. You will be surprised on how far a little consistent action will take you.

I decided at the beginning of 2013 that I would do ball-handling drills for basketball every single day. I planned on doing one hour of drills each day. As the year went on, I added more and more drills and different techniques. I also added listening to motivational tapes while I went through my workouts. All of my innovations proved to pay off as I saw more results. By the end of the year, I was doing two-and-a-half hours of ball-handling drills each day. Acting on a little plan will take you further than you think. Sometimes all it takes is a first step.

All you have to do is create an itinerary for each day that is in line with your long-term goals and follow that plan. Write down what a successful day would look like, a day of extreme progress. This will be classified as your "goal routine." That is the day that you eventually want to make into your routine. Most people make the mistake of trying to jump right into their goal routine and then burn out because they can't handle it all. Look at the day that you are living each day currently. Implement little things into your current daily routine that are easy to handle and gradually build those things up to your goal routine. You can't change too much about what you do without changing who you are first.

Make sure your actions don't contradict your desires. There are some people who say that they want to achieve things but never take action to go after those things. Common examples of these are, "I want to quit smoking," or "I need to lose weight." If you desire to change a bad habit or addiction, you can't just desire to change it and not take action. For instance, if you want to stop drinking, then attend a support group, make an effort to talk to someone who's gotten through it, or work on changing your Brain

Match. To be a great baseball player, you can't just *say* that you want to be a great baseball player; you must take action to make it happen. Do the simple things each day to propel you towards what you desire.

Look at an icicle. It did not start as an icicle. It started as a drop of water that was frozen, and it grew and increased in size with each frozen drop. Drop by drop, it became something incredible.

Don't just focus on immediate change. Focus on development.

Boredom

Doing the same thing over and over every single day, even if you love what you do, can get repetitive and boring. Many people recommend taking time off, and that can be effective, but some people can't afford to do that because they don't have much time until they have their opportunity to make their dreams become a reality. There are three effective ways to solve this issue and refresh your state of mind.

Overcoming Boredom

1. Do something different each day
2. Change the way you do things
3. Change your atmosphere

Doing something different each day doesn't mean changing up your whole routine every single day. It simply means to alter one part of your routine or add something new and unique to do each day.

Doing little things differently can make what you do more fun and challenging, and less repetitive. We all crave growth and change, so this modicum of change spices up your routine and can be the push to provide the extra motivation that you need to get over the boredom hump.

Changing the way that you do things can boost your progress. Almost always, you can change the things that you are doing in order to produce a similar result. For example, if you work out by running on the treadmill every single day, and you are starting to become bored and your progress plateaus, maybe try the elliptical for a week. That can change the way you feel when you work out, change your perspective on how you work out, and even influence the effectiveness of your workout by using different muscles and a different motion.

Sometimes when you get anxious to go through your daily routine and it gets boring, it is due to the repetitiveness of the atmosphere. That can consist of the time of day, where you do things, and who you do them around. Using the same example, if you usually work out in the evening every day after work, maybe if you started working out in the morning, then you would be refreshed and boosted. If you run on a treadmill every day, maybe switch to running outside one or two days a week to change the scenery and add excitement to your workouts. Also, if you always run alone, maybe try running with a friend to have someone to talk to and enjoy it with. You and your friend will also support each other, and they will dramatically enhance your motivation to do those things that were getting boring.

Boredom happens to almost everyone. It is a normal feeling. It doesn't mean that you aren't passionate about what you are doing or that you've lost your drive.

My dad coached my all-star baseball team when I was in little league, and we would have practice about five days a week. He would sometimes do a light practice with a water balloon fight at the end or a home run derby to make things more fun and change up the repetitive routine. This relaxed all of the players and sparked our interest in practice. My dad understood the concept that you work harder and more effectively when you change up your routine and mix up the atmosphere every once in a while.

In the book, *The Circle Maker,* author Mark Batterson says, "A change in scenery often translates into a change in perspective. A change in routine often results in revelation. In formulaic terms, change of pace + change of place = change of perspective."

Mentors

Another way to help you as you work toward your goals is to find mentors. Mentors are people you can learn from who have a certain skill that you want to attain or are strong in an area that you want to be stronger in.

There are all different kinds of benefits to having mentors, and you can certainly have more than one, so that you can work with different mentors on different areas of development. You want to talk with your mentors often and develop close, trusting relationships with them, so that you can better work together and share ideas.

You want mentors who have experience in the area that they are mentoring you in. That way you can trust that they know what they are talking about and will be able to help you when you get further down the road. It is easier to take someone somewhere that you have already been. For example, if you are having someone mentor you in basketball, would you rather have a former professional or just an avid NBA fan? That's a rhetorical question. Obviously you would want the former professional.

You can also have mentors that you don't know personally, such as an author or a professional musician. You can study their ideas and how they do what they do and learn from them. One of my favorite quotes is by John C. Maxwell. He says, "We teach what we know and reproduce who we are." The people that you choose to have as your mentors will teach you what they know, and you will start to become more and more like them because of it.

When someone asks for you to mentor them in a certain area, don't feel obliged to say yes. You can tell someone that you don't want to be their mentor if it doesn't fit into your purpose or is too time consuming. Commitment and time are required for effective mentorship. It is a privilege to be a mentor, but at the same time, it must be something that you have a passion for and something that's going to make you happy. Teaching is the best learning, so any chance that you get in life to teach someone something that you've learned, it will help you ingrain that material in your brain and actually make you more knowledgeable in that area.

With all of this information in mind, why would you *not* ask Jesus Christ to be your life mentor by learning from *His* teachings?

Commitment

A real decision is measured by the fact that you've taken new action. If there's no action, you haven't truly decided.
—Anthony Robbins

The number one reason people fail is because they go into what they do expecting failure. You must go into everything that you do expecting to succeed. Success when working toward a goal is a battle between you and yourself, it's a battle of the mind.

If you go into a race expecting to lose, then you will have a lesser chance of winning. When the race is close and you are near the front, you will have the mindset that you aren't supposed to win, and you will hold yourself back from winning, consciously or unconsciously. If you have the mindset that you deserve to win and should win, when the race is close, you will naturally take over and have a better chance of winning because you believe that first place has your name on it.

You've probably heard someone fail and then exclaim, "I knew that would happen!" That is a perfect example of someone expecting to fail. If you know that you are going to fail, and you aren't going to give it your best effort, then failure is inevitable.

Whether you think you can, or think you can't, you're right.
—Henry Ford

If you are trying to lose weight, stop trying; you must be *committed*. Don't set a goal and *try* to achieve it; instead, commit to achieving it. Trying won't get you out of the bed in the morning, but commitment will. Commitment to your goals will prevent you from hitting the snooze button on your alarm clock.

The secret to waking up early in the morning is commitment. When you commit to your goals, it will not give you a choice whether you get to hit the snooze button and roll over or get out of bed. Your commitment will force you to get out of bed. When your alarm goes off for work or school, you don't have the option to press snooze. Commit to your goals the same way.

When you set your alarm at night, you make a commitment to getting up at that time. Don't leave the decision hanging as to see how you will feel in the morning because chances are, after you wake up from a deep slumber, you won't decide to get up and do "optional" work. I've learned through my own experiences that if you don't make definite commitments, and you just live by how you feel, most often you will cop out and pick the easy road, such as sleeping in instead of getting up early.

For example, let's say that you usually get up at 6:00 in the morning to get ready for work by 7:00. If you want to start getting up at 5:00 every morning to run before work, commit to waking up at that time. Whether you have to go to sleep an hour earlier or rest at another part of the day, commit to your plan of action.

Commitment in this particular scenario would mean getting up at 5:00 every morning and making that particular time a staple for when you get up. Instead of 6:00 being your staple time to get up and having the running being a bonus thing, make getting up at 5:00 the staple. Then, make anything else bonus. Get up to run as if it is getting up for work. When you commit to what time you are going to get up, there is not a decision to make each morning. 5:00 AM is the time you must get up because you are committed to that goal and that plan of action.

If you think that commitment to a goal seems difficult and unrealistic, or you don't have the time or energy to do that, then you need to reevaluate your goals. If you set goals that you love and are passionate about, then committing to them should be an easier choice. Remember, you will make time for the things that you love.

Success is not for the weak and uncommitted.
—Eric Thomas

Another way to stay committed to your goals is to get an accountability partner, someone who will keep you accountable for doing what you say you are going to do.

Plans fail for lack of counsel, but with many advisers they succeed.
—Proverbs 15:22 NIV

Get one of your friends to meet you at the gym in the morning. This way if you think about skipping, you are not only letting yourself down but also that other person. As accountability partners, you must check up on each other and keep each other accountable to your plans of action. You can also bounce ideas off each other and see what's working for the other person and share with them what you think they should try. You can compare and contrast what is working and what isn't. It is also nice to have someone there with you during the struggle. When you are not seeing progress or face a failure, these are the people who will pick you back up and work through it with you.

You can have many different accountability partners, a group, or just one. It's all about personal preference and what you decide is best for you. You don't have to have an accountability partner, but they are very valuable, so I think that having some sort of accountability partner is almost vital to your success.

Although you obviously can have similar goals to your accountability partner(s), you don't have to. You can simply share ideas with each other on how you are implementing your own plan of action, and how you can benefit each other in different ways on your journeys.

In my own life, I have a group of accountability partners. My group consists of my brother and a couple of my cousins. We are driven in different directions for our own goals, but we are very valuable to each other's success. We inspire each other each and every day. We have a group text message that we send each other inspirational pictures and quotes in daily. Also, we call each other every now and then to check up on how we are doing and hold each other accountable to what we said we were going to do. We share our goals and our daily routines so that all of us can bounce ideas off each other and help each other any way that we can. It really is a special thing to have these people in my life, and I value them a lot. Without them, I would not be the person who I am today, and I would not be as driven to follow my dreams as I am. My group of accountability partners helps me to commit to my goals, and I do the same for them. They are some of the most important people in my life.

Stop making promises to yourself and to God that you are going to change; instead, make commitments. Commitment to God's plan for you through your goals and dreams is beyond important. That is what plugging in your life is all about.

Commit to the LORD whatever you do,
and He will establish your plans.
—Proverbs 16:3 NIV

Fall in Love With the Process

As you now know, living out of love is one of the most important components to living a fulfilling life. A way of doing that is simply to fall in love with the process of getting to your goals and dreams. The process is what you have to go through in order to see your goals and dreams come to pass: this includes your training schedule, setting goals, overcoming failures and obstacles, talking to people who build you up, and things like that. The process is how to take what the world throws at you and make something positive out of it. It is where opportunities are created. The process is the input and output of your hard work in life. By doing one thing, the process provides you with a result. By falling in love with the process, you can learn and understand how it works and how to use it to your advantage.

The process to succeed at what you want is easily hated because success requires hard work. Not many people like to get out of bed earlier than usual. Not many people like to put all of their effort into one area and take themselves out of their comfort zone. However, if you learn to love these things, then success will be a generous road, and you will do the great things that God has put you here to do.

Everyone has a unique way to achieve their different goals, so therefore everyone's process differs. Fall in love with your plan of action and what you do every single day. Fall in love with the person that you are becoming. Fall in love with everything that happens in your life, knowing that it is all for your own benefit.

When you wake up in the morning, you should have a smile on your face and be looking forward to acting out your plan of action. Even thinking about your little successes each day should give you butterflies in your stomach.

Falling in love with the process is not that complicated. It can be done two different ways. One way to fall in love with the process is by Brain Matching The Pain Theory. If you focus on your goals and getting to a place that you love instead of focusing on the pain that you have to endure and the things that you don't want to do, then things will be easier for you, and your motivation to do those once tedious things will be increased.

The other way to fall in love with the process is to live with an attitude of gratitude. If you are grateful for all of the opportunities that you have, the things that you get to do, the day before you, the relationships that you have, and you make a habit to recognize these things every day, then you will be grateful for the process thereby learning to love it at the same time. Thankfulness births love.

Similar to loving yourself in order to love others, you must love your goals in order to love the process. If you aren't passionate about what you are striving for, then you simply cannot love the process of getting there. Some people live their lives scared of the process because of their past failures. It is important to know that the process will never hurt you. You simply get out what you put in. The fear of the process hurting you is a feeling similar to that of dating someone. If you have your heart broken in the past, you might fear falling in love again until you work back into it.

In the same way, failure sometimes prevents people from picking themselves up and trying again.

The process works if you work it. If you love it and learn how it works, then it will show you love in return by giving you opportunities and improvement. That exchange of love is how success happens. You can learn how the process works by learning from failure and success. When you fail, you can look back at your schedule to see why you failed, and you can do the same when you succeed.

Staying in love with the process is the easy part. If you keep progressing toward your goals and dreams, and you begin to make a habit of progress through the process, the process begins to become your friend, and you learn how to use it. When you become familiar with the process, you will learn the causes and effects of your actions. By knowing those causes and effects, you can make a more accurate plan of action that will lead you to success.

For a simple example, if you are trying to lose weight, you will learn from the process that if you eat a hot dog instead of a salad, you will gain weight. By learning from this cause and effect, you will know to choose the salad next time. When you learn from your mistakes and failures, the process becomes more familiar to you, and you will start to see less and less failure and more success in your life.

By learning from your mistakes and keeping God as the center of your life, the other integral components of your life fall into place to guide you to living your life fulfilled and with purpose.

Excuses

Excuses are dangerous. They can give us an easy way to avoid the things that we don't necessarily want to do, even if we must do those things in order to achieve our goals and fulfill God's plan for our lives.

Greg Plitt, American fitness model and actor, said in one of his videos on *YouTube*, "If you failed, at least you tried then. 'I failed' is 100 times more of a man than 'what if,' because 'what if' never went to the arena."

Many of us sit around wondering, "What if?" What if I would've stuck to that program that I had? What if I could be a professional? What if I had more money? What if I could achieve my dream? The truth is that you can be anything that you set your mind to. I bet you just skimmed over that last sentence because you have heard it so much. Go read it again and let it sink in this time. It is a scary thought for some people to be told that they are capable of anything because they are aware of their potential, but they make excuses for why they can't achieve their dreams.

Les Brown, the motivational speaker, once said that people are afraid to chase after their dreams for two reasons. One reason is because of the fear of failure, and the other reason is because of the fear of success—that they won't be able to handle their dreams if they achieve them.

The fear of failure is an understandable fear. Nobody wants to hope for something and then fail; however, it is all about how you Brain Match that failure. As you now know, failure is a stepping stone to success when you begin to learn from your failures and improve because of them. God promotes you with every failure, and He will never make a mistake. He will always guide the way and be by your side. God will be with you through every failure and every success.

Have I not commanded you? Be strong and courageous.
Do not be afraid; do not be discouraged, for the LORD
your God will be with you wherever you go.
—Joshua 1:9 NIV

Change your Brain Match from failure being a setback to it being a stepping stone. This will help you to not fear failure but rather embrace it and therefore be fearless when setting out on the journey to achieving your goals and dreams.

Failure = Setback
DELIBERATELY CHANGED TO
Failure = Stepping Stone

A setback is a setup for a comeback.
—Eric Thomas.

The fear of not being able to handle your success also makes sense on the surface. Overwhelming success can be hard if you aren't capable of handling all the responsibility that comes with it. However, there is a big part that you are missing when you fear success. Right now, you may not be able to handle that success that you are striving for, but on the road to success, the obstacles in your path, the trials and tribulations that you must go through, the heartbreak, they all mold you into a person that can handle the success that you seek. Although right now you might be afraid that you can't handle the success you desire, you will be able to handle it once you get there.

Excuses are always available to us, and the world creates them for us. These excuses consist of things such as a mindless TV show, social media, and other people asking us to do things. All of these can cause us to make excuses to not do what we planned out to do.

An easy and effective way to beat procrastination and to overcome the habit of making so many excuses is to make a to-do list. This can be a daily, weekly, or even monthly list. Maybe, if you tend to procrastinate often, you have to put times on your to-do list that tell you when you have to do certain things. If you are a really bad procrastinator, give your accountability partner your to-do list as well. That way when that time comes, you are held accountable to do the thing that you chose to do before the day started.

For example, if getting up at 5:00 AM is on your to-do list, then you might get a call from your accountability partner at that time. If you don't answer that call, imagine the guilt that will set in. That could fix your problem right there. Creating a daily, weekly, or monthly to-do list will help you to organize all of the things that you want to accomplish in that time.

When you are committed to goals that are in line with God's eternal purpose for you, no excuse is worthy of holding you back from pursuing them. When you want something bad enough, no excuse will be big enough that it can hold you back from working towards it.

If you really want to do something, you'll find a way. If you don't, you'll find an excuse.
—Jim Rohn

Excuses are all around us, and if you look for them, I promise that you will always find them. The key is to stop looking. Don't look for an excuse to not do the things that will help you to achieve what you want to achieve and transmit God's Grace. If you want your goals and dreams badly enough and commit to making them come to pass, the rest comes with relying on God.

Jesus looked at them and said, "With man this is impossible, but with God all things are possible."
—Matthew 19:26 NIV

Positive and negative thoughts are always going to be there. It is what you choose to embrace that makes all the difference.

An old Cherokee is teaching his grandson about life. "A fight is going on inside me," he said to the boy.

"It is a terrible fight and it is between two wolves. One is evil—he is anger, envy, sorrow, regret, greed, arrogance, self-pity, guilt, resentment, inferiority, lies, false pride, superiority, and ego." He continued, "The other is good—he is joy, peace,

love, hope, serenity, humility, kindness, benevolence, empathy, generosity, truth, compassion, and faith. The same fight is going on inside you—and inside every other person, too."

The grandson thought about it for a minute and then asked his grandfather, "Which wolf will win?"

The old Cherokee simply replied, "The one you feed."

Which wolf will you decide to feed? Which one are you feeding now?

Respond to God's Will

But if you are led by the Spirit, you are not under the Law.
—Galatians 5:18 NIV

Have you ever had a feeling that you should do something or wanted to do something but didn't have the courage to take action? Your life will be raised to the next level when you start to decide to do the things that you want to do instead of those things that you are told by society to do.

Sometimes we are afraid to do things that we really want to do or have a feeling that we should do because we are afraid that it will change our reputation or make us look foolish. Other times we just don't want to put forth the effort to do what we truly want to do.

The truth is, God gives us promptings to do things all of the time through the Holy Spirit. I like to call these promptings *nudges*, because it is as if God is nudging us to grow by giving us an opportunity to expand and express our faith. Whenever you have that feeling in your gut that you should do a good thing, it is God nudging you. Sometimes the nudges that God gives us are uncomfortable. They push the limits of what we are comfortable doing. We will say that we want God's Will and not our own, yet why then would we put limits on what we are capable of and try to stay within our comfort ranges? If you make the decision to let God's plan be done in your life, then don't put limits on what you are capable of, do not fear, and do not stay within your comfort range because God has everything under control, and He will take care of all of the details of your life.

When God nudges you, He is showing you extra little things in life that you can do to grow in faith and bring Him glory. As you grow in faith, you will reach out to do bigger and better things, and God will continue to guide you His way.

God is patient, and He loves you. Although He encourages you, He will not push you further than you are willing to go. He will always be by your side, but He will not intervene and change things until you let Him.

The LORD himself goes before you and will be
with you; He will never leave you nor forsake you.
Do not be afraid; do not be discouraged.
—Deuteronomy 31:8 NIV

Sometimes life can be tough, and we can fear all different kinds of things; however, it is important to face those fears head on in order to let God's Will be done in your life. Don't run *away* from your fears, instead run *to* them clothed in the full armor of God.

I am afraid of heights. One summer, however, I went to an amusement park with my girlfriend. We were determined to face my fear of heights by going on some different rides. She is not afraid of heights, so that helped her to help me overcome my fear by making me feel more comfortable. We started off by going on some easier rides, such as a scrambler. Then, we went on a small wooden roller coaster (my first real roller coaster), but I was ok. I wasn't out of my comfort zone yet, but then we pushed my limits. She persuaded me to get in line for a swinging ship called the Sea Dragon. I stopped halfway through the line, looking up at the ride, and I told her that I didn't want to go on. She pushed me right to the point where she was not forcing me to go on, I still had a choice; however, she still tried hard to convince me to go on the ride. We watched it go through once and then decided to go on, but we sat in the middle so we didn't go up as high as the other seats. When the ride began, it was moving slowly, and I was anticipating for it to reach its peak. When it was right at my limit, I was ready to be done, but the ride kept swinging higher and higher. It pushed me to a point of panic. I could not look at anything but the bar, and I had my sweaty hands squeezed to that bar with a death grip. My bottom would come out of the seat at the top of each swing. Eventually, the ride calmed down, and I got off. Although I didn't have a desire to go back on the ride, I now had a sense of pride and achievement.

After we got off the Sea Dragon, we walked by the Sky Ride, which is a ride where you sit in a cart with your legs dangling high above the park. It is similar to a ski lift. My girlfriend asked me if I wanted to go on it, and I didn't even have to think in order to say no. We went on a couple of fun rides on the grounds, got some ice cream, and then thought about the Sky Ride again. Each time I looked at it, it looked more and more manageable. After a little while, we really analyzed the ride. I eventually worked up the willpower to get in line and take on the challenge. Once we got on, there was no going back. The ride was going to be about 5-10 minutes long. I was relaxed at first, but we kept rising higher and higher ... and higher ... and all I could see were the small people below me and the thin wire carrying me towards the clouds. I was scared, uncomfortable. As we got to the halfway point, I felt more confident because I knew that I was handling it well. I had no idea what was in store ahead. At the highest point of the ride, we began to move even slower and came to a complete stop. We were in the air with our legs dangling at the highest point of the ride! If you are afraid of heights, you can imagine the uncomfortable feeling that I felt. My girlfriend didn't address the issue, instead she continued to talk to me regularly and ask me questions about my day. I tried not to panic. We were stuck in the air for about five minutes before the ride started up again. I eventually made it to the end and got back on the ground. I was pushed way beyond my limits, but it was all ok in the end, and I was happy that I made the decision to go on the ride.

Nothing bad happened out of my fear. I didn't think I could overcome my fear and go on the rides, but I did. The good but scary thing about a ride is that once you start, you have to follow through; there is no going back. When you commit to getting on a ride, it is a commitment to all of the anxiety, pain, and change that it might bring you; but in the end, a stronger version of yourself will come out of it.

In the same way that you commit to going on a ride, you must commit to your goals. View it as if there is no other option but to develop into a person that can handle the process and the end of the ride will bring you fulfillment. You might not think that you can handle the journey right now. You might not know what it will look like, causing a feeling of uncertainty, and it might be out of your comfort zone, but a better and stronger version of yourself will come out of the journey. You won't discover how attached you are to comfort until you ask God what you should do and you hear the answer.

God will be your guidance along your journey. He will push you, but He won't force you. He will guide you, but He will not do it for you. He will never give you more than you can handle with Him, and if your faith is in Him, then He will bring people, opportunities, and obstacles into your life at His divine time. Obstacles are easier to overcome when you are assured it will all be ok in the end, so no matter what kind of pain or fear you experience, you can be assured that everything will be ok at the end of your ride because God has promised you security and shows you that throughout your journey.

No test or temptation that comes your way is beyond the course of what others have had to face. All you need to remember is that God will never let you down; He'll never let you be pushed past your limit; He'll always be there to help you come through it.
—1 Corinthians 10:13 MSG

Plugging in your life means to be willing to do those things that scare you so that you can fully let God impose His Will on your life. What if your fears are a gateway to your success?

Do one thing every day that scares you
—Eleanor Roosevelt

Go for the "Goal"

The type of goals that you set reflects the type of person that you are. Be daring and set goals that will change the course of your life, develop who you are, and keep you on the pathway to success in line with God's purpose for you. Setting and striving to achieve your goals provides you with purpose and direction. That sense of purpose and direction is essential to living a fulfilling life.

7

Be Yourself

Who are you, a mere human being, to argue with God? Should the thing that was created say to the One who created it, "Why have You made me like this?"
—Romans 9:20 NLT

God created you a certain way to fulfill a specific purpose. You are a work of art, handcrafted by God. If He wanted us all to be the same, then He would've created us that way. He gave us all different families, different looks, different interests, and different purposes for a reason. Embrace who you are, and be yourself in this world that wants you to be anything but yourself.

Becoming the True You

The more we let God take us over, the more truly ourselves we become—because He made us. He invented us. He invented all the different people that you and I were intended to be... It is

when I turn to Christ, when I give up myself to His personality, that I first begin to have a real personality of my own.
—C.S. Lewis

When you give yourself and all that you love up to God, things start to work perfectly in His plan. He created you so that He could work through you, so when you give yourself up to Him, all of your unique talents and abilities shine to their fullest.

If you get a suit tailor-made for your own use, and someone else wears it, it won't fit them properly. You made the suit so that you could wear it, and it fits to its best when you wear it because it was made to be worn by you. It is the same with God. You are God's tailor-made suit. If you try to be anything else but what God wants you to be, then you are not being used for your full purpose and potential, and you aren't living life to its fullest.

Giving yourself up to God by plugging in your life is the only way to become the best version of yourself. You will be the full you only when you let God take control of your life.

Impact Of Society

It is dangerous to be concerned with what others think of you, but if you trust the LORD, you are safe.
—Proverbs 29:25 GNT

When we are children, we all have these wild dreams of what we want to be and who we want to become. Some kids say that they want to be a professional athlete, a singer, an actor, or have their own TV show. These dreams most often die out because of what society tells us.

Society impacts who we are in many different ways. Some people strive to obey the status quo day in and day out. They want to be cool, have the newest things, and be like the most famous people. Society is capable of confusing you to be lost about who you are and what you are capable of. Your friends can even influence you to dress a certain way, play certain sports, and do things that you don't even want to do. Peer pressure is a very real thing, and everyone, young and old, is influenced by it daily. I think Paul describes perfectly what plugging in your life means in this regard in Galatians 1:10 when he says, *"Am I now trying to win the approval of human beings, or of God?" (NIV)*

Many people don't step out and be themselves because of fear. Some people fear that they will lose their friends if they are who they want to be, and other people fear that their life will dramatically get worse. But if you really think about it, being who you want to be and doing things that you want to do will bring you more joy, right? You will feel more relaxed and have a better attitude about life in general.

If you just be yourself, the right people will come into your life. You will make new friends. That's not to say that you will lose your old ones either. Those who truly support you and are your friends will stand by you through it all. These are the people who you want to attach yourself to anyway, right? Think about the people in your life that no matter what will stand behind you in every decision that you make. These are the people who are always there to help you in the rough times and celebrate you in the good times. Appreciate these people, because these are the people who will still be there for you when you make the decision to let go of all of the pressure, plug in your life, and just be yourself.

In life, you will sometimes not get to pick the people who are put around you. Because you are influenced so much by the people who are around you, that can be a challenging situation to deal with. Brain Matching people in this situation is not always the best thing to do because if they are going to affect you in a negative way, then you don't want to give them a positive connotation.

When you have to work around people who you don't like, you must do your best to avoid them and ignore them. Don't feed into what they have to say, just pay them no mind. However, when you have to work *with* people who are pessimistic and who you don't like, that is a different story.

You can't just ignore people who you have to work with. You must learn how to work with people who aren't good for you to be around. You do this by focusing on the task at hand. Don't get off subject with them talking about life and how they are having a rough time, how they are going downhill, and how work stinks—keep them on topic. If they start getting off topic, reel them back in and focus on the task at hand. Let them go complain to other people, but don't let them fill your head with that negative outlook.

Have you ever seen someone famous start doing something new, and then everyone else follows? That is because we all strive for appreciation. As humans, we crave three things: to be appreciated, to grow, and to be loved.

Appreciation, some people think, is bred by attention. Some people seem to think that they will feel appreciation and love when people notice them and when they do things that draw attention to them. That is why some people always try to make the funny joke, talk loudly so that everyone can hear their conversations, and act out. This can sometimes make people look silly, but it is because they are craving love and appreciation.

Most often people who receive more love and appreciation from their families, friends, and colleagues tend to have closer relationships in their life and develop better relationship skills. These people tend to act out less and crave attention less than those people who don't receive as much love and appreciation.

Those people who crave attention may have good reason to think that attention will give them a sense of being appreciated and loved. Maybe they have an unstable home environment, or their parents never listen to what they have to say. Maybe they just crave for someone to listen to them and love them. As you now know, love cannot be received fully if you don't love yourself and if love isn't given. If you crave love from others, the solution is to simply love yourself, give love, and appreciate love, as I talked about in the "Living out of Love" chapter.

This world sometimes tries to take your imagination away and make you come back to "reality." The so-called realists of the world are actually people who just haven't embraced the truth that you can do anything with God because you were perfectly designed to be one of a kind.

Everyone is a dreamer on the inside. Everyone has an imagination waiting to run wild and dreams to be chased. Embrace that feeling and chase those dreams because the "real world" is a phrase used by people who refuse to embrace the fact that they can achieve their God-given dreams. You were not made to live by the status quo. If we were all made to live the same way, do the same things, and live the same lifestyle, then why were we all created differently? Why do we have different dreams, different talents, and different abilities? You were made for more.

Never let your imagination be overwhelmed by society. Anybody who has ever done anything monumental has faced opposition. Some people will try to tell you that you can't do something just because they can't, but they don't know you like you do. You know who you are and what you are capable of. Go out and get what you know you deserve.

Be the hero of your own story that woke up today.

—Joe Rogan

The Pursuit of Holiness A.K.A. "You" Decisions

Happiness is not extrinsic based on this world, but intrinsic determined by your faith in Christ. Every day you should be happy regardless of your circumstances. The teaching pastor of Southeast Christian Church in Louisville, Kentucky is Kyle Idleman. I've referred to him multiple times in this book because he is very straightforward and provides accurate information regardless of how he thinks people will respond. I like what he says regarding happiness: "You don't deserve to be happy. You deserve to go to Hell… but Jesus saved you, and *that* should make you happy." Because of this salvation, Idleman explains, "When things don't go how you want them to, you are a spiritual billionaire ringing your hand over ten dollars." Happiness is found only in the death and resurrection of Jesus Christ and, like all things in this book, it is an authentic response to God's Love for you. God wants you to be happy, but happy through His Son—because that is where the only true happiness is received.

Idleman gives an explanation of where true happiness comes from in one of his sermons, and it is similar to this: Our culture says that happiness is truly from pursuing pleasure, is based on circumstances, fueled by comparison, comes from focusing on yourself, and is found by chasing; but God says that happiness comes from pursuing holiness, is based on Christ, fueled by gratitude, comes from focusing on others, and is received by faith in Christ. Happiness comes from pursuing holiness.

By making big decisions based on your pursuit of not happiness, but holiness, you will experience true happiness. Keep that in mind when the term *"you" decision* is used. A "you" decision is a term used to describe a decision following *the pursuit of holiness.*

The pursuit of holiness is not about doing what makes you *happy*; it is about making decisions that are *best* for you. Don't make decisions based on the happiness of others;

meaning, don't do things that aren't good for you just to make other people happy. Giving others joy is best done when you are happy yourself. This doesn't mean to deny God when making difficult decisions and chase happiness through pleasure, but instead to focus on God's Will and follow Him *because* you know that pursuing God's plan will make you truly happy in the long run. "You" decisions are decisions that are God's best for you regardless of your circumstances or the people around you. Those are the decisions that will make *you* happy in the long run because you pursued holiness over immediate pleasure.

Let each of you look not only to his own interests,
but also to the interests of others.
—Philippians 2:4 ESV

God wants you to do what is best for other Christians around you, but that all starts by being happy yourself. The happiness effect is similar to The Cycle of Love. If you do things that make you happy by pursuing holiness, then you will be happy about more things and be able to fully share that happiness with others. Making decisions that make you happy is not selfish. The people who care about you want you to be happy, so trying to make those people happy by doing something that isn't good for you is contradictory. Sacrificing your holiness in order to give others happiness is not doing much good to anyone.

You will thank yourself in the long run if you make decisions that are based on your own personal holiness, in turn happiness, and others will thank you as well. No matter if these are big or small decisions, they will lead to more joyful and intimate relationships later on.

In my freshman year of high school, I wasn't really pleased with the school that I was attending. It is a school that I highly regard with excellent academics, great athletics, and considerate teachers; however, it just was just not the right fit for me. I looked at other options of schools that I could attend and decided that I wanted to consider going to the school that my brother attended and where my dad is a teacher and athletic director. With family in the school, it would be more convenient, and it would set me free to be whoever "Hunter" was. With a lot of prayer and hard thinking, God steered me to make the transfer. It was a decision that set the true me free and changed my life forever. I simply followed my pursuit of holiness.

What you are doing may be good, but the good
is bad when there is something better.
—Kyle Idleman

As I attended the new school, I quickly figured out that this was a place that not only could I just be myself, but I could create myself. My beliefs were enhanced, and my faith was made stronger because of the switch. The new school provided an environment that I could flourish any way that God wanted me to.

The transfer was not easy, and I lost many friends because of it. I had a reputation that was changed and many things that I knew I would miss; however, had I not made the switch of schools, I don't really know what kind of person I would be. I am frequently asked if I made the right decision about switching my high school. I always respond by saying that I can't say that if I would've stayed, things would be better or worse, all I can say is that they would be different, and I am happy with my decision. All I knew is that the decision that I made, despite anyone else's opinion, was what God wanted for me and is what would make *me* happy in the long run, and it did.

Many are the plans in a person's heart, but it is the LORD's purpose that prevails.
—Proverbs 19:21 NIV

It is very important to pray and have God guide you through decisions that you make; however, there are sometimes big decisions that we have in front of us, and we aren't sure which way God wants us to go. It is in these situations you must understand that no matter what, "it is the LORD's purpose that prevails." God can use different situations, different people, and different circumstances to shape you and guide you in fulfilling your purpose. Instead of stressing over big decisions, pursue what you think will lead to holiness in your life, and God will use that situation to bring you joy and wonderful opportunities. My papa once said to me, "You won't always make the best decisions, but you must make the best of the decisions that you make."

Sometimes in life, you have to make the formidable decision. It might be the decision that will initially frustrate others, disintegrate friendships, and change how people look at you, but if it is what will lead to *your* holiness, then that decision is the decision that must be made because in the long run, more people around you will benefit from your happiness. Have a hunger for the presence of God, not the approval of men. That is what a true pursuit of holiness is all about.

Seek His Will in all you do, and He will
show you which path to take.
—Proverbs 3:6 NLT

Your Motivation

There are two types of motivation. One type is intrinsic, and the other type is extrinsic. These two types of motivation determine a lot about ourselves, our beliefs, our efforts, and the way we think.

The first type of motivation is intrinsic motivation: the motivation is originating from inside you, your heart. This motivation consists of things like personal growth, sense of achievement, fulfilling your purpose, and mostly things driven by love. Intrinsic motivation is important because it creates your inner drive. Your passion is fed by your intrinsic motivations. Your intrinsic motivations are the things that get you through the rough times and help develop you as a person. They reflect who you are and influence your character, so you want to have intrinsic motivations that are powerful and effective. These motivations can be empowered by listening to motivational speakers, actively participating in church, talking to people about your motivations, reading books like this, and by attending different seminars. Your intrinsic motivations will start to create who you are and have a dramatic effect on the progress you make toward your goals.

Extrinsic motivation is very different than intrinsic motivation. Your extrinsic motivations come from the outside world. Examples of extrinsic motivations are wealth, your goals, health, family—things like that. Extrinsic motivations are tangible in that you can measure them and physically see them. You can feed your extrinsic motivations by putting up pictures of what you desire or by visualizing achieving your dreams.

You can also have extrinsic motivators: people who motivate and inspire you to achieve your dreams. Your extrinsic motivators can be people such as family members, mentors, or other people who guide you along your journey and inspire you. Extrinsic motivations are the motivations most commonly thought about by people, and they are the motivations that commonly get you off the couch and striving toward your goals. Extrinsic motivations *get* you going, and intrinsic motivations *keep* you going.

Recognizing both your intrinsic and extrinsic motivations is important. Create a list of them so that you can visually see them and focus on them whenever you need to. Motivations can be developed by your own thoughts and experiences or simply placed in your heart by God. Learn to embrace your motivations and use them to your advantage by reviewing them often.

Motivation varies from person to person. Nobody is motivated by the exact same things. Everyone is unique; however, we are all driven by something. That is what makes us achieve all different kinds of our own greatness.

Defining Your Own Success

If you don't define your own success, other people will define it for you. They will tell you that you can settle for less, and they can influence you to give up as well.

When you do something good, some people around you will praise you for it and tell you how great and successful you are. If your success is not defined by you, then you might begin to settle for less than what you could've achieved if you would've kept pushing forward.

When you fail, some people will also put you down and tell you that you are a failure, and you might believe them as well. However, if your success is defined by you, then you will know that you can do better and have more motivation to strive to be successful at whatever it is that you do. Sometimes you need people to help you see more of the potential that you have, but ultimately your success must be defined by you.

Defining your success is one of the most important principles that you need to apply when you decide to plug in your life, set goals, and start to become who you were designed to be. When you know what will make you successful, it will provide you with more self-pride, help you focus, and bring more joy to your life.

It is important to define your success, but don't let your success define you. Life isn't defined by what you do, but by who you belong to—God.

What Defines You?

"Don't let a game define who you are; let the way you live your lives do that." That's a quote said by a coach from the movie, *When the Game Stands Tall*. The movie, based on a true story, is about a football team from De La Salle High School who had a 151 game winning streak that lasted twelve years. Eventually, they lose a game. The coach's quote portrays something deeper than football.

If I asked you to define yourself, what would you say? You might say something like basketball player, construction worker, video game designer, singer, artist, teacher, or something of that nature. However, your job and hobbies don't define who you are. If you define yourself as a football coach, and you lose every game of the season, then does that mean you are a poor person? Of course it doesn't.

The way you live your life is what defines who you are. If you live your life full of love and compassion for others, then that defines who you are. If you are inspiring others to follow God's Will through different areas of your life, then that defines who you are.

The way you live your life is also a reflection of your character. You've probably heard that the true you is reflected by how you handle hard times, and that is the absolute truth. When you find strength through Christ in the midst of a hardship, it develops your character and shows who you truly are.

> *You cannot look intense suffering in the face without making the choice between faith and cynicism. It either hardens you or melts you.*
> —*Brett Harris*

What is character? Is it how you treat others? Is it how nice you are or how well you handle adversity? I believe character is perfectly defined by Andy Stanley in his book, *Louder than Words*. He explains, "*Character is the will to do what is right, as defined by God, regardless of personal cost.*" Doesn't that make good character the basis for your life? Character is everything. Regardless of what you want personally, God knows what is best. Accepting and living by that fact is true character.

Society often labels people. It's not easy to think for yourself and know who you are while society is trying to tell you what group you belong in and what you are capable of. *You* determine who you are, and you are a child of God.

You will become who you think you are. If you believe the negative things that others say about you, then you will become what they say. You will start to fit into other people's mold because that is where you think you belong even though you are capable of much more. Plugging in your life means to know that God made you perfectly in His eyes, and it means to have the faith to do what He says and develop good character and high self-confidence. Your confidence in life reflects who you are in Christ.

Your will to do what God wants you to do, regardless of what it costs you is what defines who you are. What defines you is not what you do for work, your friends, or your social status—it is what you do with what you have in front of you. The extent to which you surrender your life to God's Will defines who you are.

Live in The Now

Everybody's got a past. The past does not equal the future unless you live there.
—Anthony Robbins

In our pasts, we have had good times, hard times, and all sorts of memories. Your past is important because you are a reflection of every single one of your yesterdays. Every action that you have taken up to this point has developed who you are, and each choice that you have made has developed your current circumstances, goals, relationships, activities, and habits.

Some of us have had rougher pasts than others. Getting over a difficult past is definitely a process; however, choosing to follow that process is a decision you must make in order to live joyfully. How you feel about a negative past will not be made positive accidently; it takes deliberate effort and time.

Many people will try to forget their past and think that they can overcome it that way. Trying to forget your past will just build up all of your feelings and frustration inside of you, and you will never live your life truly free and fulfilled.

To get over your past and your bad memories, you must embrace what has happened to you. You must embrace the wrong choices you have made, the bad habits you have created, and the negative relationships that you have developed. If you don't like your current circumstances in life or who you have become, then you are not stuck there.

One way that you can face your past is to write down how your past decisions and events have made you feel and influenced your life. Seeing the areas of your life, habits, and qualities that you have acquired due to your past and embracing where they came from will help you to determine why things really are the way that they are. From there, you can deal with those problems. You can talk to the people who you must talk to in order to develop and change those relationships that are affecting you negatively. You can realize and change the negative Brain Matches and habits that you have developed by visually seeing and figuring out why they were created in the first place. Seeing your past visually on paper and seeing how your current life circumstances came to be will help you to realize what you need to change in order to live in the now and move forward in a positive direction.

Another way to face your past, if you are already aware of what events or decisions have shaped who you are and your current situation, is to let out your feelings. Instead of letting all of your frustration and pain build up inside you, having it control your life and the way you live, you need to let it all out. Whether this means talking to the people who affect your life directly, crying out for God to show you guidance, writing your feelings down, talking to a friend, or just crying to yourself, you must let all of your feelings out. This will make you feel better and help you to move on with your life and live in the now.

We do not have the excuse of ignorance, everything—and I do mean everything—connected with that old way of life has to go. It's rotten through and through. Get rid of it! And then take on an entirely new way of life—a God-fashioned life, a life renewed from the inside and working itself into your conduct as God accurately reproduces His character in you.
—Ephesians 4:20-24 MSG

A bad past can control your life now, and it can also determine where you are headed. Bad events, relationships, and decisions from our pasts are not the only things that can control and have an effect on our lives and current situations. Our *good* events, relationships, and decisions from our pasts mold us in many ways as well. Sometimes we have great success after great success and become satisfied with where we are. From here, we feel like we have "arrived" per se. Your past successes don't mean that your purpose in life is fulfilled, because the purpose that God gives you here on earth is a limitless mission. If you are still alive, then God has more for you to accomplish. God has a way of taking your past mistakes and using them to create future blessings.

Being successful and achieving great things is obviously going to affect the way you live your life in a positive way, but you still have to live for today. Regardless of past circumstances, failures, or successes, you only have today, and it is necessary that you make the most of it.

> *You are where you are because of who you are.*
> *And if you want to be somewhere else, then you*
> *are going to have to change something.*
> —*Eric Thomas*

Don't let your past determine your purpose. Don't let your past set your goals. Don't let what you were born into or past circumstances bring you down to a standard that is less than what you are capable of or make you strive for something that you aren't passionate about. You have special talents and abilities to make a difference in the world. You are not your circumstances or your past. Those things do not define who you are. Your past is not the determining factor for what you are capable of.

If you have failed in the past at something, it doesn't mean that you aren't capable of doing it. If you commit to achieving a goal that you love, then you can certainly accomplish it.

Sometimes we let our parents, where we grow up, and the cultures in which we are raised determine the reality our lives. I like what Joel Osteen says: "You are not defined by your past. You are prepared by it." Some people try to fit into the mold that their past has made for them; however, each day is a new day, and you have a choice on how you want to live each moment. Today, develop a better version of yourself. Begin to move forward in the direction of your goals and dreams, not the so called "reality" around you, but your own dreams. Each and every day, change the course of your life and create a new past.

Today determines your tomorrow, meaning that where you are today was determined by what you did yesterday. Whatever you do today, the things that you achieve and the progress that you make, those things will carry over to tomorrow. The decisions that you make and the habits that you develop today will carry into your future. You will gradually become what you do each day. Aristotle said, "We are what we repeatedly do. Excellence, then, is not an act, but a habit." Your circumstances are produced by your daily decisions. Life is filled up with a bunch of todays—not yesterdays, not tomorrows, but todays.

We are products of our past, but we don't have to be prisoners of it.
—Rick Warren

Tomorrow doesn't exist. Every day will always be *today*. If you live for *today*, do your best *today*, do things you love *today*, and make decisions that give you joy *today*, then every day will be a day that you gave your all to. If you make decisions every day that give you joy and do things that you love, then you will live a joyful life doing things that you love. It really is that simple. Living joyfully *today* is a key to living a life of fulfillment.

Andy Andrews wraps up this concept nicely in his book, *The Seven Decisions*. He says, "The past will never change. But you can change the future by changing your actions today. It is really a very simple process. We, as humans, are always in a process of change. Therefore, we might as well guide the direction in which we will change."

Therefore do not worry about tomorrow, for tomorrow will worry about itself. Each day has enough trouble of its own.
—Matthew 6:34 NIV

Your Own Definition of Normal

Normality is self-judged. There is nothing in life that can be classified as "normal" by everyone.

Many people mistake average to be the same as normal. In almost every thesaurus, normal and average are synonyms. That is a Brain Match made by society, and it must be discarded from your brain. If you Brain Match normal and average, then you are most likely living an average life or view yourself as average. Normal is defined by your lifestyle. Some things that you do every day might seem normal to you but extraordinary to someone else.

A bodybuilder might think that it is normal for someone to lift *three* days a week. Being a bodybuilder, they lift six days a week. They view themselves as above normal in that area, obviously. A video game designer's view on exercise might be *one* day a week, so what is normal? Is it normal to work out one day a week or three? It depends on your lifestyle. That video game designer might deem that it is normal to play video games for at least an hour a day, but the bodybuilder thinks that it is normal to play one hour of video games per year! Through this example, you can see that normality is based on personal definition.

Your definition of normal can be changed as you grow physically, spiritually, and mentally, and also as you become a better or even worse (hopefully not) version of yourself. I used to think that getting up before 7:00 in the morning was an aberration, but as I have grown, set new goals, and developed new aspirations for my life, I started to realize that 7:00 AM is too late to be getting up for all of the things that I want to accomplish each day. The normal time I got up used to be at around 7:20 AM. Now, my normal time to get up is about 5:30-6:00 AM. My normal was changed as I developed into a better version of myself and set new goals.

Normality is not something that we strive for. Most of us strive to be above the standard of normal at something at least. We all have our niche and maybe normality is what you strive for in those areas that you aren't very strong in. That's ok, because your definition of normal is a benchmark that you can work different areas of your life around.

What is "normal" as a Christian? Is it normal to pray every day? Is it normal to go to church every single Sunday? Is it normal to read the Bible every night? Is it normal to spread the gospel? These are things that can only be determined by you and also by the guidelines of Scripture.

The Bible doesn't tell us exactly how we are to worship God. God doesn't say, "Everyone worship Me by playing sports," or, "Everyone worship Me by singing songs." He has obviously given us guidelines on the way to live our lives and shows His Grace in our lives by guiding us to live His way, but the freedom of Christianity is that we all have different ways of worshiping God and spreading His Word. That is the beauty of life.

There are many different "normal" ways to live life as a Christian. We can all worship God differently, and you must begin to be accepting of all of the differences that people have and the different definitions of "normal" that everyone creates.

My challenge for you is to raise your standard of what is normal in your life.

Your Attitude

Your attitude, not your aptitude, will determine your altitude.
—Zig Ziglar

Attitude is everything. Your attitude determines your successes and who you are as a person. Your attitude day in and day out becomes a habit.

Attitudes are contagious; is yours worth catching? As you know, you become most like who you surround yourself with. In this same respect, the people who are around you become more and more like you. When you have a positive attitude, the people around you will start to "catch" that same positive attitude. By developing and having a good, positive attitude, you will experience more success in life, and the people around you will experience that success as well. If you have a negative, bad attitude, it will work the same way. You can catch bad attitudes as well as give them to others. A bad attitude will result in more frustration in life, and a pessimistic outlook will draw more things to you that will cause you to be frustrated and agitated.

Bad company corrupts good character.
—1 Corinthians 15:33 NLT

Surround yourself with people who are positive, as I have talked about in the previous chapters of this book, and you will develop that same positive attitude. This will also benefit the people around you as they develop that positive attitude as well. The people who catch that attitude from you will then spread it to others. Attitude has a rippling effect. Attitude is the most contagious, life-changing virus. If you have a positive attitude, others will develop it as well. Then, you, as well as others that catch the attitude that you have, will experience more success and joy in life.

Attitude is simply the law of attraction in action. The attitude that you have, good or bad, determines your response to the things that happen to you and affects the people who come into your life.

The longer I live, the more I realize the impact of attitude on life. Attitude, to me, is more important than facts. It is more important than the past, the education, the money, than circumstances, than failure, than successes, than what other people think or say or do. It is more important than appearance, giftedness or skill. It will make or break a company … a church … a home. The remarkable thing is we have a choice everyday regarding the attitude we will embrace for that day. We cannot change our past … we cannot change the fact that people will act in a certain way. We cannot change the inevitable. The only thing we can do is play on the one string we have, and that is our attitude. I am convinced that life is 10% what happens to me and 90% of how I react to it. And so it is with you … we are in charge of our attitudes.
—Charles R. Swindoll

Feeding your mind

Your eye is a lamp that provides light for your body. When your eye is good, your whole body is filled with light. But when your eye is bad, your whole body is filled with darkness. And if the light you think you have is actually darkness, how deep that darkness is!
—Matthew 6:22 23 NLT

This world is full of negative influences that will cause you to have a pessimistic outlook on things that happen to you, so you must ignore these influences and be circumspect about what you feed your mind. As I stated in the "Brain Matching" chapter, you must be careful of who and what you surround yourself with because those things will dramatically affect your life. If that means eliminating social media from your life, then that's the sacrifice that you have to make in order to live purely and fulfilled.

In psychology, The Law of Exposure says that our lives are determined by our thoughts, and our thoughts are determined by what we are exposed to.

You cannot have a positive mindset when all you feed yourself is negativity. When you are in the car, instead of turning on the famous rap station, turn on the Christian radio station. When you listen to negative, ungodly music, your brain begins to reflect the negative aspects of that music. The good news is that positive music and encouraging messages work the same way.

When someone comes up to you and starts to talk badly about someone else, spread a rumor, or tell you what someone said about you, it is not a bad idea to politely tell them that you don't want to hear it. Don't fill your mind with that trash. Who cares what people say about you? All that matters is what you say about yourself and what God thinks about you.

In every encounter we either give life or we
drain it; there is no neutral exchange.
—Brennan Manning

Jealousy can control our minds if we let it. People sometimes tend to get jealous when they see others succeed. Everyone wants success, so when we see others achieve it, jealousy begins to creep into our minds. Don't let that jealousy control your mindset. Paul says in Romans 12:15, *"Rejoice with those who rejoice, weep with those who weep." (ESV)* God wants you to be happy for people who succeed instead of getting jealous, and He wants you to show compassion for those people who are struggling rather than judging them. To deny jealousy and judgment from entering your mindset and to let compassion and joy control it instead is an expression of true faith.

You can't let negativity slip into your mind because a negative mindset will cause you to live with lower self-confidence and unfulfilled potential. When your life is plugged into God's Will, positivity and joy flow into your life and overwhelm you.

I heard once that you should strive to be a thermostat, not a thermometer. A thermometer is determined by its circumstances, but a thermostat determines its own circumstances. In life, don't let your natural circumstances determine who you are, instead strive to be a thermostat and determine the circumstances around you.

You are what you eat, so feed your mind what you want to become. No matter how much you exercise your faith, your strength is ultimately determined by your diet.

Illumination

You can tell what they are by what they do.
—Matthew 7:16 CEV

We are all born with different purposes, different goals, different talents, and different dreams. We look differently, act differently, and talk differently. We all have different pasts and aspire for different futures. That is the beauty of mankind. You have special gifts and an eternal purpose put in you specialized by God.

When you walk into a place, people should know what kind of person you are and what you do or stand for without you even having to say anything. What God has instilled within you should illuminate from you; however, you will only illuminate if you are plugged in. Who you are will only be conspicuous if you are plugged into the purpose God has given you. When your heart matches up with God's eternal purpose for you, magic happens. That is when you start to illuminate.

If you are not plugged into God's eternal purpose for your life, then you are simply an unplugged TV. Your life and the things that you do and achieve become transient. When you are plugged in, however, all of God's Grace, Love, and Mercy will flood into your life. That is when who you are can start to illuminate from you. Your picture appears to everyone on your screen, through your life.

Look at a bodybuilder, and at first glance you will know what they do. Who they are illuminates from them. You can physically see their hard work and what they love.

We all know at least one person who comes into a room and lights up that room. Their happiness exudes from them and spreads to everyone around them. They provide energy and excitement by doing everything with purpose. God wants you to have that same kind of effect on people in your own way by embracing who you are.

You don't have to physically show anything or wear any special clothes or outfits in order for who you are to illuminate from you, but your presence alone should tell people who you are. God wants us to be proud of who we are because He made us perfectly to fulfill His purpose for us.

People admire what you take pride in. For example, if you are an artist, people will admire you for that and maybe even Brain Match you with your art. Take pride in who you really are through Christ, and be proud of what you love to do because people will admire that and be inspired to do the same.

In the last section, I explained that your true character shows in times of struggle. In this section, I am challenging you to let who you are show all of the time! God has made you perfectly the way He wanted. You are a perfect version of yourself.

Illuminating who you are by plugging in your life to God is similar to Batman's Bat Signal. The Bat Signal is a light that shines into the air for everyone to see. The light in the sky has the Batman logo on it. However, without any light, the Bat Signal is useless. Your character is the Batman design. In order for your character to illuminate from you, you must have your life plugged in so that God's light can shine through you, and who He has created you to be can illuminate from you.

Yourself

This world and everyone around you might try to mold you into something that you are not, but you know within yourself what brings you joy and who you really are. It's time for *you* to stand up for what *you* believe in, pursue holiness, do things that bring *you* joy, and change the world *your* God-given way. Let God do His perfect work through you so that you can become all that you were meant to be and accomplish all that you were meant to accomplish. Simply, *be yourself.*

Be yourself; everyone else is already taken.
—Oscar Wilde

8

A Life of Faith

Faith is the substance of things hoped for,
the evidence of things not seen.
—Hebrews 11:1 NIV

Faith is something that you *must* have in order to live a fulfilling life. Without faith, you are simply nothing, pursuing nothing because you don't believe that you are capable of more.

"Faith is the substance of things hoped for." What does this mean? It means that when things are intangible, when they are not yet a reality and unable to be physically seen, faith is our way of making them tangible. Some people believe that seeing is believing, but when you can't see things, such as God or a dream that you are committed to, faith can take the place of that tangibility, and it can be the visual or physical substance that you need in order to believe.

"...the evidence of things not seen." This part of the verse pertains to evidence. According to Dictionary.com, *evidence* is defined as, "that which tends to prove or disprove something; ground for belief; proof." Evidence is just proof that something is true. The verse from Hebrews says that faith is the proof of things not seen. Faith is proof that God, your goals, and your dreams are real and proves them to be true. In order to have faith in something, you must create an image or substance to have faith in. That substance is evidence that what you have faith in is real and true. To summarize this concept, when you have complete faith in something, it makes what you have faith in real and true to you.

It's not that you must see it in order to believe it; it is that you must believe it in order to see it.

Faith in God

The pastor of McLane Church in Edinboro, Pennsylvania is Brian Kelly. In a sermon series titled, *Vertigo*, he introduced the three steps of faith needed to obtain salvation by studying Paul's letter in Romans. I found this concept very interesting and applicable. This section is based off his sermon series, and I will share the three steps of faith that he shared and some of his principles on faith in this section.

It is through faith that a righteous person has life.
—Romans 1:17 NLT

Pastor Kelly brought up a good point: Have you ever seen ads on TV that advertise things to help you lose weight or to do certain things in life easier? These products are usually scams, but people still buy them. Why would people buy these products if they know that they are ineffective? It is because we are all looking for anything we can find to help us with our everyday struggles in life.

We were created for Heaven, but so much of this life misses that reality. People sometimes use the expression, "Life is Hell right now." This expression proves true in that this life can be like a Hell to us sometimes if we separate ourselves from God. That is because God is everything Hell is not, so the further away from God we venture, the more "Hell" we will experience in our lives.

If you live your life God's way and fulfill His plan for your life instead of your own, then you will experience more little moments of "Heaven" in your life.

Salvation is rescue from a broken and meaningless life both now and in the future. How do you get rescued from this meaningless, broken life? Salvation is not obtained by a determined commitment to self-help, but with a humble request for God's help.

Salvation is obtained through your faith. Salvation is determined by one decision to repent and do things God's way, but it is the faith that you must build up over time in order to have the strength to make that life-changing decision. Pastor Brian Kelly concluded that there are three things that you must do in order to demonstrate faith and obtain salvation.

1. Acknowledge your problems
2. Know that God *always* has the solution
3. Do what God says

Acknowledging your problems means to recognize and accept that you are not perfect. You face problems every day when you wake up in the morning. Everyone has problems, and everyone is a sinner. Knowing your problems is the first step to solving them. Sometimes what we think is the problem is not the real problem but instead a symptom of the problem. These symptoms won't go away until the real problem is resolved.

Pastor Kelly gave a great example of this concept. Let's say that a child is doing poorly in school, so his parents punish him for it because they think he is being lazy. They take away TV, his video games, and ground him from going anywhere with his friends. The child keeps getting punished, but his grades don't improve. Eventually, they find out that the reason their child is doing poorly in school is because his eyesight is bad, and he can't see the board. The problem was not the child's effort, but his sight. That is a great example of why knowing the root of your problem is important. By knowing your problems and taking care of them through God's answers, the symptoms will be taken care of as well. Don't focus as much on your problems as you do on the solution—God.

Plugging in your life means to recognize that God has the answer to every one of your problems because He is perfect. Because of this, you want to do what He says in order to solve your problems. If you would trust anyone else, why not trust God?

Pastor Kelly gave a great example for this step as well. Let's say that you think you broke your leg, for example, and you are in a lot of pain. You go to the hospital, and they tell you to elevate and ice it so that you can get the swelling down before they check it out. Are you going to refuse to do that and say no? What if you think that it won't help? Are you going to do it your own way? No, you are going to listen to what the doctor says because he is the expert. This leads me to this question: If you will have faith in the doctor to do things his way, then why don't you have the faith to do things God's way? Why do you try to do things your own way when God tells you differently? Isn't He the expert?

Mark Batterson says, "Many people believe that they are following Jesus, but they have mistakenly invited Jesus to follow them." You cannot do things your own way and live a fulfilling life. What if an owl, which is nocturnal, decided to sleep at night instead of during the day? It wouldn't work out well for the owl because that is not how God designed it to live. In the same way, sometimes our lives don't work the way that God has intended because we try to do things our own way. We try to replace God with earthly things or people when we don't live completely for Him. We think that we can give our own life purpose and meaning, and we invite Jesus along for the ride.

God gives us eternal life through His Grace, and we were put on this earth to glorify Him and lead others to do the same. When we don't put God in the center of our lives, our picture of reality becomes distorted because our necessary faith in God is missing. This leaves us confused and not sure about what to do or where to go because we refuse to accept God's plan for our lives.

If you believe that God has the answer to *all* of your problems, then you will *want* to live the way God wants you to live and obey what He says, as you believe that a doctor has the answer and you acquiesce to what they say. You will want to live that way because it is the only truly fulfilling way to live. Corrie ten Boom says in her book, *The Hiding Place,* "If you look at the world, you'll be distressed. If you look within, you'll be depressed. But if you look at Christ, you'll be at rest."

Since what may be known about God is plain to
them, because God made it plain to them.
—Romans 1:19 NIV

This piece of Scripture from Romans is simply stating that people know the truth about God because He has made it plain and clear to them. Jesus explained how God wants you to live, did He not? We all have the Holy Spirit, do we not? God has made things plain to us. Life is just a matter of deciding to do things His way.

Behind everything, there must be someone. This is a law of nature, a way of the world. Look at everything invented. It all was once someone's idea, and then it was their creation. Look at this book for example. It was my idea to write this book, and then I created it. Now the words that you are reading are here. They didn't just appear out of nowhere.

Another example is the iPhone. It didn't just one day appear in the universe. It was thought of by Steve Jobs and then created. Behind every creation, there must be a creator, so let me then ask you this question: Where did the ground come from? Whose idea was the sky? Whose idea was this Earth? Whose idea was man? If all things fall under that rule, nature cannot be an exception. The "someone" in those questions is simply God.

The problem, however, is what we've done with that conclusion. Could it be that in the places you are struggling or areas that are weak in your life exist because you have moved God out or not fully embraced His plan for you in that area? Are you trying to figure out the creation without consulting the Creator? Maybe that is why the road is bumpy at times. To have true faith in God is to embrace His plan for all areas of your life and to truly live for Him, knowing by the substance and evidence of your faith that He will provide you with things greater than you could ever imagine and show you true Grace, Mercy, Peace, and Love.

At times it seems as if God has abandoned us, like He is not there. You pray and have no response. You don't see Him acting in your life. This happens sometimes during the most arduous times in our lives. Plugging in your life means to know that God is always working behind the scenes even if you don't notice it, and that at His divine time, He will reveal His perfect work in your life.

Sometimes God lets us try to handle situations on our own to test our faith, and other times He waits for us to let go of trying to do things on our own. God is jealous when it comes to your heart, and He wants you to realize that the things of this world fall far short in comparison to its

Creator, and when we refuse to listen to God, the only way He can do that is to let us figure it out on our own.

But when envoys were sent by the rulers of Babylon to ask him about the miraculous sign that had occurred in the land, God left him to test him and to know everything that was in his heart.
—2 Chronicles 32:31 NIV

This verse refers to God leaving Hezekiah. However, God did not leave him entirely. "God left him to test him . . ." When God tests your faith, He does not just go away and leave you alone. God stays by your side always. He sometimes just lets you handle situations on your own to test your faith and mold you into a person that can handle His favor.

I used to wonder, if God can do anything, why He would let bad things happen. It doesn't make a lot of sense for God to make us experience bad things if He loves us so much; however, my girlfriend said to me once, "If you could handle everything, then what is the point of faith?"

That simple question proves true in every aspect of life. If God only gave us things that we could handle, things that weren't overwhelming and didn't stretch our faith, then we wouldn't really need God would we? God gives us no more than what we can handle *with* Him. Sometimes He gives us things that we can't seem to handle on our own, and it overwhelms us. This is simply to make us stronger and amplify our faith. What is a big deal to us isn't always a big deal to God. He understands what a big deal really is, so He will work things out in your life according to the full picture. If you have plugged in-type faith in God, you will not be overwhelmed, stressed out, or taken over by the difficulties of this world. If you let God take the wheel and have utmost faith that He will work everything out for you and work through you, then life will begin to be less stressful and more fulfilling.

Each decision that you make is a test of faith. When you make a decision that demands omnipresent intervention, you are expressing true faith.

Faith is the substance to which we can fully begin to understand the Grace of God. Sometimes what you believe will be slightly different than what others believe, and that's ok. Paul says in Romans 14:1-3, *"Accept other believers who are weak in faith, and don't argue with them about what they think is right or wrong. For instance, one person believes it's all right to eat anything. But another believer with a sensitive conscience will eat only vegetables. Those who feel free to eat anything must not look down on those who don't. And those who don't eat certain foods must not condemn those who do, for God has accepted them." (NLT)* It's ok to be open to what other people believe and accept what they believe, but you must also stand firm in what you believe. Don't change what you have faith in due to what others believe around you unless they open your eyes to a new perspective. Share your faith with others and know in your heart and soul that God is with you wherever you go, watching over you and taking care of you because He loves you. You are His most valuable possession. Remember this principle: when your faith stretches, so do your dreams. Embrace the substance or image that your faith creates, and you will achieve dreams more immense than you could ever imagine.

In the book, *The Purpose Driven Life,* author Rick Warren explains that God has an unchanging nature. There are many things that you must know about God and praise Him for in order to understand His unchanging nature. Here is a list of those things found in the book of Job:

- That He is a good and loving God: Job 10:12
- That He is all-powerful: Job 36:22, 37:5, 23
- That He notices every detail of my life: Job 23:10, 31:4
- That He is in control: Job 34:13
- That He has a plan for my life: Job 23:14
- That He will protect me: Job 5:11

Relationships and Faith in People

I have been at the bedside of many people in their final moments, when they stand on the edge of eternity, and I have never heard anyone say, "Bring my diplomas! I want to look at them one more time. Show me my awards, my medals, that gold watch I was given." When life on earth is ending, people don't surround themselves with objects. What we want around us is people—people we love and have relationships with. In our final moments we all realize that relationships are what life is all about.

—Rick Warren

A relationship is the most important thing on this earth to develop because relationships are eternal. Developing strong, intimate relationships is essential to living a life of fulfillment. These kinds of relationships are the kind that you would have with a family member, your spouse, or a close friend. To develop these types of relationships, you must have faith in people.

Don't you feel good when you know that you can rely on someone to do something for you? For example, if you tell your friend to keep something that you tell them private, it is nice to know that they will. It is nice to know that if you need someone to talk to, you can rely on a close friend and know that they care about what you have to say.

It Is Better To Have a Friend

You are better off to have a friend than to be all alone, because then you will get more enjoyment out of what you earn. If you fall, your friend can help you up. But if you fall without having a friend nearby, you are really in trouble.
—Ecclesiastes 4:9-10 CEV

If you can't trust anyone and have no faith in people, then you will struggle in the midst of a crisis. We all need succor at times, and the ability to trust people is very important in attaining that assistance and support.

An important thing to understand about faith in people is that it is fragile. An example of faith being broken would be a person committing adultery. This is a severe example, but it demonstrates my point very well. Their spouse will really have trouble trusting them again, and there is good reason for it. This kind of lost faith will result in huge damage to that relationship, in this case, most often a divorce. Because of this faith in a person being broken, the person who was cheated on will most likely never trust a person fully in that situation again. This is due to the Brain Match of marriage with the pain of being cheated on.

How do we get our faith in people back once it's broken? The reconciliation of faith in someone is quite simple on paper. The truth is that you have to change your Brain Match of the situation. You must see that situation as pure again instead of uneasy; however, if someone that you had faith in broke your trust, then it's probably not a good idea to trust that person with very big things again right away. Forgive them as Christ has forgiven you, and then start trusting them with small things. From there, you can build back your trust in them gradually until that faith is restored. Trust is built, not given.

Don't tell someone that you will do something if you aren't committed to doing it. False words damage faith. Be a person that others will easily develop faith in, and that will develop relationships of shared faith to build those strong relationships that are needed in order to live life fulfilled. Being a person who is easily trusted is done by effectively communicating. If a relationship has poor communication, the trust in that relationship will be a reflection.

God wants us to develop relationships with each other and love each other. We were never meant to be alone, which is why He created Eve in the first place. We get lonely sometimes, and that shows us that we need and love being around people. Relationships and love are the most important things in life, because those two things are eternal and praise God more than anything else in all of His creation.

But if we walk in the light, as He is in the light,
we have fellowship with one another, and the blood
of Jesus, His Son, purifies us from all sin.
—1 John 1:7 NIV

Faith in Yourself

DO YOU BELIEVE IN YOURSELF?

The man without self-reliance and an iron will is the plaything of chance, the puppet of his environment, the slave of circumstances. Are not doubts the greatest of enemies? If you would succeed up to the limit of your possibilities, must you not constantly hold to the belief that you are success-organized, and that you will be successful, no matter what opposes? You are never to allow a shadow of doubt to enter your mind that the Creator intended you to win in life's battle. Regard every suggestion that your life may be a failure, that you are not made like those who succeed, and that success is not for you, as a traitor, and expel it from your mind as you would a thief from your house.
—Orison Swett Marden, An Iron Will

When you take action on your desires, you are demonstrating faith. Faith in your goals and dreams is essential to achieving them. If you don't believe that you can achieve your dreams, then you never will. Success is never an accident. It only happens from hard, intentional, consistent work.

When you have faith in yourself and your abilities, your self-pride is augmented, and you will feel better about your capabilities. You will work harder towards goals that you believe you can achieve than those that seem way out of reach. Don't let this be because of the size of the goal, but because of the size of your faith.

On the journey to your goals and dreams, there will be negative people and events that will try to make you feel like your goals and dreams are impossible and that you aren't capable of achieving them. Plugging in your life means to know within yourself that you can do anything with God, and that you are most definitely capable of making any dream come to pass that you are passionate about.

If you let life and people tell you what you are capable of, who you are, and what you can achieve, then you will become depressed because this world is negative to those who don't belong to it—those who belong to Heaven. People naturally like to build themselves up by putting others down, sometimes without even knowing it. Remember that you were chosen by Jesus to come away from this world. You do not belong to this world, but to God.

The world would love you as one of its own if you belonged to it, but you are no longer part of the world. I chose you to come out of the world, so it hates you.
—John 15:19 NLT

Remember, your goals and dreams have your name on them. You are the only one who can achieve your dreams, your way. When you start to become competitive about your dreams and think that someone else can take them away from you, you are losing faith and deceiving yourself. Keep your mind focused on *what* you can do, not *who* you can out-do. Competitiveness toward your dreams will most often cause you to think that you aren't good enough to achieve them because you will naturally overestimate your competitor and underestimate yourself. This will cause you to get more down on yourself with each failure. That is why many dreams that are very achievable don't come to pass for people.

Your dream is yours and yours only. The only thing standing between you and your goals and dreams is your beliefs. The failures, tough times, getting out of bed early, doing things that you don't particularly want to do, they are all battles between you and yourself. Have faith in yourself and know that you control your own destiny. It's *your* dream. All you have to do is go out and get it.

It may seem like the world is spinning out of control at times, but you are always stabilized when you fix your eyes on God. God intends everything He does to happen. He is perfect, and we are imperfect. Therefore, we need Him in order to achieve our dreams. Because our dreams are in line with God's plan for our lives and are to bring Him glory, we need Him to walk with us on the journey to achieving them.

In the difficult times, when you find yourself with little faith, in the midst of ebb, it is important to know that "the tide always comes back." God is placing more big opportunities in your path right now. Take advantage of the little opportunities that you have each moment so that when the tide comes back, you are ready to set sail.

In the movie, *Facing the Giants*, one of the actors tells this story: *"There were two farmers who desperately needed rain, and both of them prayed for rain. But only one of them went out and prepared his fields to receive it. Which one do you think trusted God to send the rain? Obviously, God sent the rain to the one who prepared his fields for it. Which one are you? God will send the rain when He is ready. You need to prepare your fields to receive it"* Prepare your field for the big opportunities by taking advantage of the little ones.

The bigger the dream you have, the more doubters you will face. People will make you aware of every little thing that will encumber you from your dreams, and sometimes you will want to believe their doubts and negative comments—especially when you don't see progress yourself.

There are three reasons that we sometimes believe the doubters in our lives. One reason that we sometimes believe the doubters is because chasing our dreams is not easy—it takes commitment and hard work—and we just want to quit and take the easy way out a lot of the time. Nobody will blame you for giving up on a wild dream. That makes it very easy to quit, and that road to give up and give in will always be there. Faith means to constantly persevere. Everyone who has ever done anything great has had doubters. Don't live a predictable life. A plugged in life is a life that demands an explanation.

The second reason why we sometimes believe the doubters and give in to what they say is because we all have a little bit of doubt inside of us when we set out to achieve a big dream that we have. None of us are 100% confident at the beginning that we will be successful. Doubt starts out as a little seed, so when people doubt us, that little seed inside of us is watered, and it grows bigger and bigger as we believe each one of the doubters. Eventually, that doubt can overwhelm our visions of our dreams and make us settle for less than what we are capable of.

The third and final reason that we choose to believe the doubters is because the doubters are sometimes people who we love and trust. These doubters could be your family, friends, your spouse, or a person that you look up to. We all want approval of our dreams and crave for someone to relieve that little doubt within us, so when we tell someone that we love and trust our dream, and they don't think that it is possible for us, then that can damage our hope and increase the magnitude our own doubts greatly.

A simple way to avoid most of these doubters is to not talk about your dream as much, but to take action instead. Just flat out work towards your dream and make it happen. You don't have to tell everyone you see about it and get their approval. If you have God's approval and believe in yourself, you can make anything happen. Remember, your confidence in life reflects who you are in Christ. Don't just have self-confidence; have God-confidence.

Don't be so naive and self-confident. You're not exempt. You could fall flat on your face as easily as anyone else. Forget about self-confidence; it's useless. Cultivate God-confidence.
—1 Corinthians 10:12 MSG

You must let God take the wheel and have faith in yourself that you can do and achieve anything you want in life because you have God-confidence. Your dreams are yours to take; your name is on them. By the Grace of God, have faith that He will show you the way.

You are capable of more than you think. Other people can prove this to you in your life.

When I got my driver's permit, on a Friday, I was excited to get driving in a parking lot over the weekend and practice stopping, parking, and a little bit of turning. I had driven in the driveway before, but that was just to back the car out of the way of the basketball hoop so that I could shoot baskets and not hit the car. I thought learning to drive was going to be difficult, and it would take some time until I could get on the actual road. However, the Friday night that I got my permit, I was going to my team's high school football game to watch because I couldn't play due to mono. I got ready to go and was about to get into the passenger seat of the car when my dad handed me the keys. He was going to let me drive! The game was about a 30 minute drive from our house (40 with me driving). I tried to plead my case to my dad that I had never driven before and asked how he expected me to drive over 30 minutes on real roads. He believed that I could do it. He had his utmost confidence in me. Although the ride was not perfect, and I made some small mistakes and a couple of bad turns along the way, the experience changed my life. I now had confidence in myself as a driver. I was better than I thought I was, and I would've never known that if it weren't for my dad's confidence in me to drive.

Faith is taking the first step, even when
you don't see the whole staircase.
—Martin Luther King, Jr.

When people put their confidence in you, your own self-confidence grows, and you discover abilities that you never knew you had because you never stretched yourself past what you thought was possible.

Without faith, our imaginations and dreams disappear, and we begin to drift through our lives instead of living with purpose and conviction. A plugged in life is a life of faith. I dare you to live a life of faith and watch as God overwhelms you with the results.

9

Purpose

Therefore go and make disciples of all nations, baptizing them in the name of the Father and of the Son and of the Holy Spirit, and teaching them to obey everything I have commanded you. And surely I am with you always, to the very end of the age."
—Matthew 28:19-20 NIV

Jesus' last words recorded in Matthew reveal the purpose of our lives as followers of Christ. Jesus says to "go and make disciples of the nations." Pay attention to how He starts off His command. He says "go." This is a call to action. Jesus was telling us that fulfilling our purpose in life requires us to *do* something. At the end of Jesus' life here on earth, He says some of the most important words in the Bible: "And surely I am with you always, to the very end of the age." Jesus gives us the purpose to spread His teachings and show people to follow Him, and the last line has great significance because He is telling us that we are not alone in doing this. This is where most people get off track. They work to develop their divine gifts and spread the gospel, but they forget that God is actually *with* them through life. Jesus' last words tell us that we don't have to accomplish our purpose alone—it doesn't all rely on us. God has a purpose for all of your life, and the only way to fulfill that purpose is to trust Him and let His plan happen by plugging in your life.

Rescue those being led away to death; hold back those staggering toward slaughter. If you say, 'But we knew nothing about this,' does not he who weighs the heart perceive it? Does not He who guards your life know it? Will He not repay everyone according to what they have done?
—Proverbs 24:11-12 NIV

Solomon wrote in Proverbs that our purpose in this life is to "rescue those being led away to death" and to "hold back those staggering toward slaughter." Slaughter refers to death, and death in this respect refers to eternal death or torture, which is in turn Hell. We must save those who are being led away to Hell by the universe, by temptation, or by other people.

The rest of the verse simply states that God knows when you truly believe in what you are doing and that you cannot fake anything. Because spreading the gospel through your passions is your purpose, and you know that it is your purpose, you will be rewarded for what you do, and you will be held accountable for all that you refuse to do as well.

God is counting on you to fulfill the purpose He has given you for your life by doing those things which you are passionate about and pursuing the dreams that God has put in your heart.

You can glorify God and worship Him in anything that you do. Whatever you love, God loves as well because He loves *you* and created everything. Everything that is created was His idea or a dream that He instilled in one of His children.

So whether you eat or drink or whatever you
do, do it all for the glory of God.
—1 Corinthians 10:31 NIV

Everything that you do throughout your whole day, do it all for the glory of God. If you have something you must do that you find menial or tedious, don't dread it; instead, do it for the glory of God because He gave you the ability to do it. See everything as the opportunity that it is rather than seeing it as an obligation.

God wants you to use your talents that He has given you to bring honor and glory to His name. If you do that, then He will reward you with a fulfilling life.

We have different gifts, according to the Grace given to each
of us. If your gift is prophesying, then prophesy in accordance
with your faith; If it is serving, then serve; if it is teaching,
then teach; if it is to encourage, then give encouragement;
if it is giving, then give generously; if it is to lead, do it
diligently; if it is to show mercy, do it cheerfully.
—Romans 12:6-8 NIV

Nobody has the exact same talent as somebody else. Talents vary because of the purpose in which each person acts on their certain talent. I am an author, and other people can be authors too. Does that mean we all have the same talent for writing? Not by a long shot. No book ever written was the same. Every author has a different message, a different voice, and a different purpose for why they write. Every basketball player has a different reason for *why* they play basketball. No basketball player plays the same. No teacher teaches the same. One teacher may be able to reach a certain student that no other teacher can, and that student could go on to become the President one day! The future President could come to be all because that one teacher acted on her specialized talent of teaching. Only God knows why you have your talents, but your purpose is to transmit His Grace through them.

Whatever you do, work at it with all your heart, as working for the LORD, not for human masters
—Colossians 3:23 NIV

God's Eternal Purpose

But His plans endure forever; His purposes last eternally.
—Psalm 33:11 GNT

Some things that seem big to us aren't a big deal to God. That is because we can't understand God's eternity perspective. If at the end of life there was only death, then people would make more impulse decisions, and there would be no reason to invest in long-term pleasure because all that would matter is the here and now. Because of the belief in life after death, morality begins to matter. It is the same with our eternal purposes. People often worry about the here and now—this life—when in reality, the work you accomplish in this life is meaningless without being plugged into the eternal purpose and plan that God has for you.

Do not conform to the pattern of this world, but be transformed by the renewing of your mind. Then you will be able to test and approve what God's Will is—His good, pleasing and perfect Will.
—Romans 12:2 NIV

We are all surrounded by people who set life-long goals and live for a life-long purpose. You must be "transformed by the renewing of your mind," adjusting your thought pattern and your perspective. By changing your perspective from a life-long perspective to an eternal perspective, your life will begin to have more meaning, and things you used to think were a big deal will begin to seem petty.

Notice How Romans 12:2 says that God's Will is "good," "pleasing," and "perfect." His Will is always for the good; it knows no evil. His Will for you is pleasing; it is fulfilling. When you are acting out the Will of God in your life, it is the only way to fulfill the craving for a purpose within you. God's Will for your life is perfect. He designed it especially for you. It is perfect to God's ultimate plan of creation and perfect in that it will bring you joy and true fulfilment as He works through you to do great things that glorify His name.

All that is not eternal, is eternally useless.
—C.S. Lewis

You might be thinking to yourself, *Well I know people who have lived their lives completely for God, but they still had bad stuff happen to them and didn't end up living a great life.* If you live with an eternity perspective, you will realize that death on earth is not the end. Eternity will reward you if you reward yourself by living for God's glory.

When you focus on your eternal purpose, some of your aspirations and temptations start to seem useless. You will discover that some of your goals and dreams might need to actually be expanded or completely changed. You might view some of your temptations as ridiculous and useless. Living your life with the eternity mind-set might change the things that you strive for and the way that you treat others as well as yourself.

The best use of life is to spend it for something that outlasts it.
—William James

God's Will for you is beyond this life. It is time that you renew your mind to eternity-thinking and plug in your life. Start doing things God's way to fulfill His good, pleasing, and perfect Will for you in your life. That is the only way to live a life of fulfillment.

So we fix our eyes not on what is seen, but on what is unseen, since what is seen is temporary, but what is unseen is eternal.
—2 Corinthians 4:18 NIV

Finding Your Way

A finite person or being cannot have purpose or meaning without an infinite reference point. That infinite reference point is God. God and His purpose for us are the reason we can be fulfilled, and they are what give our lives meaning. Without faith in God, we have no purpose.

But you are a chosen people, a royal priesthood, a holy nation, God's special possession, that you may declare the praises of Him who called you out of darkness into His wonderful light.
—1 Peter 2:9 NIV

God has allocated each of His children to do outstanding things. We all have unique dreams, unique opportunities, come from unique places, and have unique lives. God has set each and every one of us apart. You are one of a kind, "a royal priesthood … God's special possession."

When you have successes because of God acting on what seems like the impossible, you owe Him *all* of the glory because it was *His* plan for your life, and everything that you do is all because of *Him*. When you are successful and give God the glory, this shows others what God can do through them as well.

Some people confuse their job with their purpose. A teacher, for example, might feel that their purpose is to educate children. A builder might feel that their purpose is to build things. This way of thinking provides people with a limited purpose, and God's purpose for all of us is a limitless mission.

If you do what you love, your job will most often be a way to fulfill your larger purpose in life. If you follow your passion, opportunities for jobs that are in line with your purpose in life will become apparent as you develop your God-ordained skills. Your purpose follows your passions. That is how God designed you—how He designed us all. God wouldn't give you a purpose that you don't love. Being a teacher, for example, might be in line with your purpose in life to do something bigger, to fulfill a more meaningful purpose. In the case of being a teacher, maybe the bigger purpose is implementing a new way to reach students, forever changing the way people teach. Teaching may be your job, but it might be a way of fulfilling that larger purpose.

Some people see things as, "The higher paying job, the better." Some motivational speakers and life coaches don't support chasing money and look down on "money-thinking." It is important to know that they only look down on chasing money because they support chasing your dreams. If you have a dream of accomplishing something great, then you must simply do what you love, and the money will find its way to you through your passion. You might not see *how* the money will come to you, but if you do what you love, know your purpose, and trust God to provide, then the money will come.

The Money Formula

1. Do what you love
2. Know your purpose
3. Trust God to provide

Chasing money is a positive thing if it is in line with your goals or dreams. If your goal or dream is to provide for your family, or if you need the money to achieve a goal or dream in line with your purpose, then that is what you have to go after. In that case, money is a good thing to value.

Money is an element that supplements the journey to our goals and dreams. Supplemental factors are things that help supplement what you are working for. For example, if you are committed to losing weight, you might work out every day. That is your basic plan of action. A supplemental factor to your routine to help you achieve your goal might be eating a healthier breakfast. It is something that is not necessarily your main course of action, but it is something that aids you in achieving your goal.

Money is a supplemental factor to some people's goals and dreams; however, if your only goal is to obtain money, then you must ask yourself, "How is my pursuit of money in line with my purpose?" Maybe you need to reevaluate what your purpose is, or maybe money is something that helps you pursue your goals and dreams, like all other supplemental factors.

God wants you to use your special passions and talents to pursue your dreams that are in line with His purpose for you. God's favorite thing is to see His children develop the talents that He has given them and accomplish great things by following their passions. That is how you can do what you love, fulfill your purpose, and live a jubilant life all at the same time. This plugged in lifestyle is what brings glory to God.

What's Your Why?

While you are working toward your goals, people will ask you, "Why do you do what you do?" When you set out to achieve a goal, there must be a driving purpose bigger than you and your own publicity, money, or false sense of fulfillment. You must have a *why*. Plugging in your life means doing things with purpose and doing them intentionally. Your purpose answers the "Why?"

In the summer of 2014, my cousin Ian Kallay, aspiring professional triathlete, biked across the country at the age of only twenty. However, he didn't do it just for himself. He rode across the country to spread awareness for human trafficking. He had a definite *why*. When he got on his bike, it was for those children being sold as slaves.

Ian came up with the idea to ride across the country while he was on an extensive bike ride to surprise our family at a gathering the summer prior to his trip.

His *why* was because of the cruelty of human trafficking. "When I was little, I saw an amber alert on the TV and I asked my dad, 'What's going on?' and he told me that it was children being kidnapped." This has stuck with Ian all of his life up to this point. As he read more books on human trafficking and talked to people who also work to spread awareness, he has discovered that it takes place in most of our cities and towns here in the U.S. It's not just something that happens overseas, it happens in our neighborhoods every single day! Ian developed a passion for raising awareness and thought "What other way to spread the word than to do something that I love and that I have a talent for."

It wasn't easy for Ian to calculate his route, places to stay, and money for food and all of the nuances, but he put it all together because he was motivated to raise awareness. He called his project, *AXUS (A-cross the United States).*

Raising awareness for the trip wasn't a walk in the park either, but Ian started many different social networking accounts, created wristbands, sold t-shirts, and even held a banquet for the event to inform people of his *why* and to explain the logistics of his trip. As more friends and family began to become aware of the trip and cause, it had a rippling effect. This was Ian's idea from the beginning.

People were attracted to what Ian had to say because they were impressed by what he was going to do. If he would've done something that he wasn't good at to raise awareness, then not as many people would've taken interest in it. When Ian told people that he was going to bike across the country, people would ask, "Why?" This gave him opportunity after opportunity to raise awareness for the cause.

When Ian told people about his cause, this didn't just end it for them. They would be curious to learn more on their own and inform others. This was how more and more people became aware of human trafficking and contributed to the cause.

Ian's training was driven by his *why*. His *why* got him out of bed in the morning. His *why* made him go to the gym when he didn't feel like going. Sometimes Ian would sit in a chair and stare at a wall for an hour. That part of his training was to increase his discipline and patience while he was on the bike. He was truly dedicated because he had a deeper purpose behind accomplishing his goal.

As Ian set out on June 23, 2014 from Dayton, Ohio, he was making a difference by doing what he is passionate about. Ian explained to me, "When times got hard, I thought about those kids who don't have a chance and how I can be a part in giving them one." When things got hard, and he didn't want to bike anymore, he kept peddling because it wasn't about him anymore—his purpose was beyond himself.

Ian's ride took him 37 life-changing days to complete. He had 31 days on the bike with three days off. You might be thinking in your head that 31 days + 3 days = 34 days, not 37, and you are exactly right. Near the end of his ride, Ian had a pretty serious crash that changed everything. He had scrapes all over his body and a possible fracture in his hand that put him in a sling. He could not finish his journey on the bike due to safety precautions. Ian, however, being the amateur ironman triathlete that he is, was not going to be stopped. Ian decided that he would run the last 100 miles in three days, crossing the Golden Gate Bridge on foot instead of on the bike, and that's exactly what he did.

Nobody would've blamed Ian for giving up after his crash. His parents suggested that he just drive to the finish, but when I talked to Ian on the phone later on, he said, "I had to finish. I had to find a way. The pain that I was going through was nothing compared to the pain that those children go through each day." Ian pushed through and finished the journey because he had a deep purpose—his trip had meaning. He persevered because of his *why*.

Ian's trip across the country affected many people, even people who he doesn't know. Personally, I am very close with Ian, and we are accountability partners, but when he told me that he was going to bike across the country to raise awareness for human trafficking, I honestly wasn't exactly sure what human trafficking was. I had to have him explain it to me. Now, after his ride, I have a good understanding of what it is. I wear my *AXUS* t-shirt often and my *Stop Human Trafficking* wristband almost every single day. Ian has changed many people's perspectives on human trafficking in the same way that he has changed mine.

Not only did Ian's journey affect other people, it also affected Ian himself. It didn't only change his life on the outside, but it also changed who Ian was on the inside.

When I asked Ian about how his journey across the country affected him, he replied, "It demonstrated that you are always capable of more than you give yourself credit for. And I found that if I put myself in a situation where I have no choice but to finish, I will grow into that person that can finish."

Ian did not have a choice whether he wanted to continue peddling or not while he was on his journey. That was not his decision to make because he was not biking for himself. His purpose carried and drove him toward his goals.

Ian would bike four to six hours each day for around 100 miles. On his longest day he biked for 147 miles, and it took him about eight hours. Ian just kept peddling—up mountains, through deserts, and in the cold to fulfill his purpose.

As Ian describes, he had no choice but to change into a person that could conquer his endeavor. As he started out, he wasn't quite the person that he needed to be in order to bike across the country, but with each day, that person was developed to handle the next day, and the next, until he was transformed into a new person. He put himself out there to a place where he had no choice but to get on his bike each morning and pedal. His commitment to achieving this goal pushed him past his limits and broke the chains that enslaved the old Ian, and a new, stronger version of Ian emerged. He *grew* into the version of himself that could finish because the whole journey was deeper than his personal wants and just accomplishing a bike ride across the country. Ian biked with purpose in each pedal and achieved his goal because of it. He has made a difference through a purpose that matters.

Ian's story is a perfect example of how to follow your dreams that are in line with God's purpose for you, set a goal that is in line with that dream, and fulfill that dream by achieving your goal.

If you are curious to learn more about Ian's trip or human trafficking, I encourage you to visit *axtheus.com.*

So I run straight to the goal with purpose in every step. I fight to win. I'm not just shadow-boxing or playing around.
—1 Corinthians 9:26 TLB

Life with Purpose

If you don't have a purpose for your life, your goals and your dreams will not be fulfilling—something will always be missing. Without recognizing your purpose, you will always have an empty feeling inside that something is missing from your life, because it is.

If you don't have a reason for every action that you take, then why would you take that action? When you identify God's purpose for your life by evaluating your passions and live for that purpose, your life has a deeper value.

Stop and ask yourself, "What really matters in my life?" Seriously take the time to look over your daily schedule, your goals, people who you surround yourself with, your habits, the way that you treat people, and determine if those things honor God. Is your life a God-honoring life? You are the only one who can determine whether you are content with your life.

In order to live a life of fulfillment, you must live content but never satisfied. When you achieve a goal or a dream, it is important not to be satisfied with where you are. You must always be growing and expanding in order to live fulfilled. If you are satisfied, then your passions and dreams start to fade, and you begin to become complacent. When you achieve a goal or a dream, you must move to the next one, and the next one, and continue to grow and progress. Satisfaction kills imagination and destroys growth.

Successful people are always thinking ahead. Eric Thomas, an admirable high-energy motivational speaker, creates a great analogy of this concept in one of his *T.G.I.M. (Thank God It's Monday)* videos on Youtube titled, *How many moves ahead are you?* He says that life is like chess. Novice chess players think one move ahead, good players are three or four moves ahead, but *experts* are thinking around 25 moves ahead!

We all want to be on an expert level. You must make decisions off of decisions that haven't even been made yet. You must know your goals after your current goals are achieved. You must always be living in the forward. That way you are always growing and expanding your confidence, capabilities, and also your faith.

Contentment is important, because you want to be happy with where you are. You want to feel good about your life and love who and where you currently are. You must appreciate and find joy in your current circumstances in order to move forward towards your goals and dreams while fulfilling your purpose. If you aren't happy where you are now, then how do you expect to be happy when you achieve your dreams? If you aren't content with what God has given you now, then what makes you think that you will be content when God gives you more? From contentment, growth will flourish, but from satisfaction, the desire to grow will die.

Life God's Way

They exchanged the truth about God for a lie, and worshiped and served created things rather than the Creator—Who is forever praised. Amen.

Furthermore, just as they did not think it worthwhile to retain the Knowledge of God, so God gave them over to a depraved mind, so that they do what ought not to be done. They have become filled with every kind of wickedness, evil, greed and depravity. They are full of envy, murder, strife, deceit and malice. They are gossips, slanderers, God-haters, insolent, arrogant and boastful; they invent ways of doing evil; they disobey their parents; they have no understanding, no fidelity, no love, no mercy. Although they know God's righteous decree that those who do such things deserve death, they not only continue to do these very things but also approve of those who practice them.

—Romans 1:25, 28-32 NIV

Human purpose is connected to an infinite outside resource that is an external reference point. When we make something else besides God our external reference point to provide us fulfillment, such as ourselves or sin, it is called idolatry.

Sometimes we worship the things that God has created instead of the Creator Himself, and by our actions and our lives, we encourage others to do the same. That is the exact opposite of what God intends for us to do, yet we continue to do this every day by making false gods out of sex, money, our boyfriends or girlfriends, our cars, our houses, and especially our cell phones. We look for fulfillment in those things and always come up empty. They cause us to struggle with negativity, temptation, and an empty life. Everything you achieve or struggle with in your life depends on what idols you choose to worship.

When we look to anything to give our lives meaning and fulfillment except for God, we are committing idolatry. In Kyle Idleman's book, *Gods at War*, he says this: "Idolatry is the tree from which our sins and struggles grow. Idolatry is always the issue. It is the trunk of the tree, and all other problems are just branches."

As we demonstrate a life of trying to give ourselves true pleasure and fulfillment, we obliviously promote others to do the same. As we live a life of purpose while giving all of the glory to God, the people around us will do the same.

We live apart from God by living our way instead of God's way. Some people have the idea that when we sin, God takes his wrath out on us and punishes us. That is simply inaccurate.

God gives us a choice of what to live for. If we chose things other than God, then He responds by allowing us to sin and often experience the consequences. Sin is God's response, not a cause of His response. Sin seems to produce difficult circumstances, but God allows this difficulty because He loves you. God does not put fences around you to imprison you; He puts guardrails up to protect you from living a wasted life. God is not trying to keep you *from* something; He's trying to get you *to* something.

God is similar to the force that runs a street light at an intersection. If there was no light, people would be left to figure driving out on their own with no guidance as to what the best way is. If people didn't obey the lights at an intersection, it would be just as if there were none at all. Disobedience to God is just as bad as God not existing! Life works best when everyone obeys the street lights, and when people don't, it is not just going to hurt them but those around them as well. I don't like red lights, but just as a red light prevents you from disaster, God allows certain things to happen and guides you a certain way because He loves you and knows what is best for your life. No matter how many times you disobey God, just like the street light, He will never give up on guiding you in the right direction. If you run a red light, you will suffer the consequences of getting a ticket, but the light is constant—God is constant.

God is fair and just; He corrects the misdirected, Sends them in the right direction. He gives the rejects His hand, and leads them step-by-step. From now on every road you travel will take you to God. Follow the Covenant signs; Read the charted directions.
—Psalm 25:8-10 MSG

When we replace God with ourselves and our own wants, we begin thinking that we can provide our own fulfillment. We end up living a life of defiance. Because we are our own reference point in this situation, we are always right. This makes us start to live a life of opinion making arbitrary decisions rather than living a life of purpose through God's Will.

Idolatry only leads to us harming ourselves. Our sin doesn't equal God's wrath and anger, as many people have it Brain Matched. When we sin or put ourselves or anything else in place of God, He doesn't take His anger out on us or love us less, He just frees us to do what is wrong.

False: Sin = God's wrath (God is disappointed)
Truth: Sin = Harming ourselves
(God loves you the same)

When we are freed to sin, our sin becomes less than fulfilling and starts to harm us. A simple example of this is when you tell a kid not to draw on the table. When you do this, his temptation to draw on the table is stronger and gives him more adrenalin. When you free him to draw on the table, then drawing on the table doesn't provide him with as much pleasure. Also, if he knows that drawing on the table will ruin the table, then whenever he does it, he will feel bad because his table is now drawn on.

When a parent tells their child to put on a sweatshirt and a coat before going outside, they know that it is going to keep them warm. However, if the child only puts on a coat and no sweatshirt because they think that they know best, then the child pays the consequences of being cold. The parent isn't affected by this. The parent doesn't love their kid less because they didn't wear their sweatshirt under their coat, and they will forgive them for it, but the child is affected by not listening to their parent and thinking that they know better.

God is like the parent, and we are like the child. We may not think that we need to do all of the things that God wants us to, but He knows best. Plug in your life by having faith in God, because He can see the whole picture and knows better than you do. Your rejection to what God tells you to do is only doing *you* harm.

As you now know, until the problem is resolved, the symptom won't change. Until you make God the center of your life and do things His way, you will continue to harm yourself and be disquieted by things that don't actually matter.

For God chose to save us through our LORD Jesus Christ, not to pour out his anger on us.
—1 Thessalonians 5:9 NLT

You cannot live a life chasing short-term pleasure and be living for God at the same time. You cannot give your life *mostly* up to God. You must *fully* give everything up to the service of God and become a servant of the Lord. That is the only way to live a truly fulfilling life and live out your eternal purpose.

For we are God's handiwork, created in Christ Jesus to do good works, which God prepared in advance for us to do.
—Ephesians 2:10 NIV

Do all that your Lord tells you to do and know that with Him, all things are possible. God will guide you in the possible that leads to the impossible. If you are faithful, God will take it from there. If you do the possible, God will do the impossible.

Mary, faithful to God, honored Him in all that she did. When the angel came to her and told her that she would have Baby Jesus, she replied in Luke 1:38: "*I am the LORD's servant, may your word to me be fulfilled." (NIV)* Mary didn't think that God couldn't carry out His Word or doubt that it was possible for her to have a baby as a virgin. She understood that God would work the impossible in her life.

Pastor Kelly of McLane Church says that our lives are like baking a cake. You must follow the directions in order to bake your cake the right way. You can't just not use baking powder, replace sugar with salt because you think salt is healthier, or switch out butter with olive oil to reduce fat. You cannot substitute out or tweak ingredients in the recipe for your own whim based on what you want or else you will be eating a really bad cake, and you won't have the full taste that is possible.

God has the recipe for your life. You must make an honest effort to obey *everything* that He wants. You can't be half in and half out, or you aren't going to have the fulfilled potential of your life. You won't have the delicious cake that

God intends for your life if you refuse to follow His recipe directly.

Let's say a mother tells her son to clean the whole kitchen. She specifically tells him to clean the floor, the dishes, the cabinets, and the tables. The son, being "obedient," goes to the kitchen right away to start cleaning ("Delayed obedience is disobedience." —Rick Warren). When he goes into the kitchen, he starts dusting and wiping up the floor. Then, he wipes off a few cabinets, but not all of them because that's a lot of work and some are high up, and they really aren't that dirty in his opinion. Because everything else looks good enough, he stops after just cleaning the floor and the bottom of a few cabinets. When the mother comes to check how her son did, she sees that the cabinets are still dusty, there is a decent-sized spill in the corner of the counter, and there are also some dirty dishes in the sink. The job was incomplete in her eyes. The child did not fully obey his mother but rather did what they personally thought was right instead. The child's mother knew better about what needed done, and he didn't completely understand what the fullness of a clean kitchen looked like.

This is how some of us obey God's Will. It is important to be obedient to all that God says to do and not to make exceptions for things that God tells you to do because you think you know better, or because what God says doesn't make sense at the time. God knows what needs to be done in order for joy, love, and fulfillment to fill up your life and for you to fulfill your purpose. God wants you to trust Him even when you think that you know a different or easier way to do things. That is what the plugged in life is all about.

When things don't make sense and get difficult, remember that God is the master chef of your life. I don't like tomatoes. Alone, I think they taste really bad, but if you throw them in a hot salsa, they are great. You might be going through a "tomato moment" right now. It may seem difficult to understand why God is letting this phase take part in your life, but just remember that God will use this as a key ingredient to your wonderful salsa. God has more ingredients that He will use at the right moments to amplify the taste of your current life.

For whoever wants to save their life will lose it, but whoever loses their life for Me will find it.
—Matthew 16:25 NIV

Your life cannot be mostly-plugged in. If a husband is faithful to his wife most of the time, then he is not at all faithful. If you obey the law most of the time, then you are still breaking the law. You must obey the complete recipe in order to have the fullness of the cake. You can't live a betwixt and between life. If your life is half-plugged into God's Will, then it can easily be bumped out of the outlet by temptation and hardships. But if you are not just all *in* but all *out* as well, making a deliberate effort each day to live for God, then nothing can detour you from fulfilling God's purpose for your life, and nothing can come in the way of your fulfillment and joy through Jesus Christ.

It's not very easy to snap your fingers and do everything that God wants you to do. It can seem bothersome at times due to the temptations of this world and the earthly desires that we all have, but I like the way Brett Harris explains doing these hard things. He says, "We do hard things, not in order to be saved, but because we are saved. Our willingness to obey God even when it's hard magnifies the worth of Christ, because in our hard obedience we're communicating to the world that Jesus is more valuable than comfort, than ease, than staying safe."

Living life God's way to bring Him honor and glory is the only way to live fulfilled and with true purpose.

Life is like a rope. It has many knots that represent things that we love and hold on to in our lives. Giving your life up to God is like throwing that rope off a cliff—it is a sacrifice. You cannot hold on to certain knots in your life and still throw the rope. You must let go of everything in your life and give it all up to God so that He can make things better than you could ever imagine and tie the biggest, strongest knots you've ever seen.

Then Jesus said to his followers, "If people want to follow Me, they must give up the things they want. They must be willing even to give up their lives to follow Me. Those who want to save their lives will give up true life, and those who give up their lives for Me will have true life. It is worthless to have the whole world if they lose their souls. They could never pay enough to buy back their souls. The Son of Man will come again with His Father's glory and with His angels. At that time, He will reward them for what they have done. I tell you the truth, some people standing here will see the Son of Man coming with His kingdom before they die."

—Matthew 16:24-28 NCV

10

Death

One of God's greatest acts of love is letting us die so that we don't have to live forever under the curse of sin. In our souls, we all have this desire and truth that there is something transcending this life. We all have a feeling of eternity in our souls that resides inside of our being. We all have that feeling because Heaven is our home. I like the way that Rick Warren puts it in his book, *The Purpose Driven Life.* He says, "Life is just the dress rehearsal before the real production ... Earth is the staging area, the preschool, the tryout for your life in eternity. It is the practice workout before the actual game; the warm up lap before the race begins. This life is preparation for the next."

This life is to be lived for God. The importance of letting His Will be done in your life and plugging in your life is everything. This life is full of anguish and sin, but according to the The Pain Theory, beyond this pain is the greatest reward of eternity in Heaven. Heaven is greater than anything that could ever be imagined. It is incomprehensible because our imaginations don't reach far enough to understand the capacity of its perfection. It is a place with no pain, no sin, no boredom, no anger, no jealousy, no anxiety, no pressure, no fear, and no guilt—just tranquility and love forever as we all do things that we love and are reunited with our loved ones. Heaven is eternal perfection.

And God shall wipe away all tears from their eyes; and there shall be no more death, neither sorrow, nor crying, neither shall there be any more pain: for the former things are passed away.
—Revelation 21:4 NIV

Heaven is a creation of God, and it is our home. We are creations of God, finding our way to God through this life and finding our way to our eternity at home in Heaven through death. Death is not leaving the place that we have become accustomed to; it is returning to it. Death is not leaving our comfort and our home. When you die, you will instead enter into your home for eternity.

Your eyes saw my unformed body; all the days ordained for me were written in Your book before one of them came to be.
—Psalm 139:16 NIV

God knows you inside and out. He knows the time of your birth and the time of your death. He knows how you think and what you love. His eternal purpose for your life is perfectly ordained and specialized just for the way that He made you.

Do you not know? Have you not heard? The LORD is the everlasting God, the Creator of the ends of the earth. He will not grow tired or weary, and His understanding no one can fathom.
—Isaiah 40:28 NIV

What God knows is unfathomable. He knows you better than you know yourself. He knows sins you commit that you don't even know, and He *still* loves you! He is your mighty God, your Father. The question is then, why *wouldn't* you plug in your life to His Power and Knowledge?

Death is Life. When we die, we are being born back into our home in Heaven where we belong. Jesus died to eliminate our fear of death. Paul says in 1 Corinthians 15:51, *"But let me reveal to you a wonderful secret. We will not all die, but we will all be transformed!" (NLT)* Live your life on earth the best way that you can to honor God and know that death is only a gateway to your eternal life of perfection.

Death is not your termination, but your transition to eternity.
—Rick Warren

When you die, what do you want people to say? Do you want people to talk about what you did or who you were? Don't just make an impact, leave a legacy.

Temptation

This world is naturally ruled by short-term pleasure. Some people cut in line, do all sorts of drugs, get drunk every night, have sex with people who they don't even know, and use the expression, "I'm going to have the time of my life," often. People want pleasure now. Nobody wants to wait for something that they want. That is why people give up on their goals so often. People want to see instant progress and have immediate pleasure, and when they don't get that, they give up.

When you create and ingrain a bad habit into your head for many years, you can't just fix it in one week. Change is a process, as you now know from the previous chapters of this book, and change is sometimes only done when you let others into your life to help you. Some things are not meant to be handled alone, and sin is one of those things. Temptation gets weaker as you let more people into that area of your life to offer help and support. A plugged in life is not a life free of sin; it is a life without desire for it.

God knows that we have this temptation to sin and give in to short-term pleasures. You might be thinking, *God is God, He doesn't understand my human temptation and how I feel.* God didn't create us for perfection. He knows that we are sinners and that we will always be sinners until we are purified in Heaven by Him. God understands your temptation because He created you. God knows everything about you. He knows how you think, where you have been, where you are, and where you are headed. He designed you to be wonderful, and He pays attention to every footstep that you make.

He did not need any testimony about mankind,
for He knew what was in each person.
—John 2:25 NIV

If you don't believe that God understands your temptation and doesn't know how your mind works, take this example into consideration:

And the LORD God commanded the man, "You are free
to eat from any tree in the garden; but you must not
eat from the tree of the knowledge of good and evil,
for when you eat from it you will certainly die."
—Genesis 2:16-17 NIV

Notice that God says "for *when* you eat from it ..." God doesn't say *if*; He says *when*. God knew that Adam and Eve would eat from the tree because He understood their temptation. God knows how your mind works because He created you that way.

You might think to yourself, *If God knows everything that I'm going to do, then is my life just predestined?* In the Bible, Paul says a lot about predestination. The perplexing thing about predestination is that if God has predestined your life, then what is free will? Think of it like this: God knows you so well because He created you that He actually *knows* what decisions you will make in certain situations! That is how we know that God will provide us with the struggles and victories that we need in order to put us in a position to perfect our faith and determine our destiny.

It is mind-blowing to know that the Sovereign Creator of the universe is taking care of all of us individually. I was walking through a cemetery one time and started to realize that I only knew one person in that cemetery. As I looked at gravestones as far as the eye can see, I thought about how God knows every single one of those people better than anyone on earth … and that was only one cemetery.

In Hebrews 12:2, many different translations of the Bible refer to Jesus as *"the author and perfecter of our faith."* Imagine God as the *author* of a novel, and *you* as His main character. As you live your life, God is writing the book. You are who you are, and you have the free will to make your own decisions, but it is only because God designed you that way.

In the movie, *National Treasure,* does Ben Gates (Nicolas Cage) protect and save The Declaration of Independence, or is it actually Jon Turteltaub (the director)?

In *The Great Gatsby*, does Wilson kill Gatsby, or is it really the author, F. Scott Fitzgerald?

David wrote in Psalms 139:16, "*…all the days ordained for me were written in your book before one of them came to be.*" Although we have free will, God perfects our faith though the circumstances He writes for us. Your life might be difficult at times, but remember, God puts you in circumstances that always offer an escape. Paul says in 1 Corinthians 10:13, *"But when you are tempted, He will also provide a way out so that you can endure it." (NIV)* God doesn't *know* your future, He *determines* it based on what you do with the free will He has given you. I like what Proverbs 16:9 says: *"We can make our plans, but the LORD determines our steps." (NLT)*

Furthermore, because we are united with Christ, we have received an inheritance from God, for He chose us in advance, and He makes everything work out according to His plan.
—Ephesians 1:11 NLT

Temptation becomes petty when you begin to realize that God is sovereign and in control. In the book of your life, God has assured you a happy ending through the death of His Son on the cross.

Then the LORD said to Satan, "Have you considered My servant Job? There is no one on earth like him; he is blameless and upright, a man who fears God and shuns evil."
—Job 1:8 NIV

God let Satan tempt Job any way he wanted, except to lay a finger on him. That is because God knew the faithfulness of Job. The devil does not need to put those who are in his control under pressure. When you are satisfied in your sin, the devil doesn't need to try very hard to lure you because he controls you. Satan has control over you through the temptations that you give in to. That is the passage that you give him into your life. It is so important to cut that passage off. When you choose to obey God instead of sin, the devil will try as hard as he can to tempt you. That is why temptation becomes so strong when we try to change the bad things that we do. In order to change for the better, you must understand God's Will for you, and your want for His Will needs to be greater than the short-term, meaningless pleasure of sin.

Temptation is a sign that Satan hates you,
not a sign of weakness or worldliness.
—Rick Warren

After God told Satan to consider tempting His servant Job, Satan reveals something interesting. He eventually replies with this question:

"Have you not put a hedge around him and
his household and everything he has?"
—Job 1:10 NIV

Satan uses the term "hedge" as a way of something blocking his access to tempt Job. Many other translations use the term "fence" or "wall of protection." This allows us to conclude that God has some sort of protection around those who try their best to be faithful to Him—those who live a plugged in life. Because God has a "hedge" around us, blocking out Satan and his evil, we can be assured that nothing bad can happen in our lives without God's permission. No evil can cause us death or even harm without the permission of God. When you are tempted, and when things go wrong for what seems like no reason, you can be assured that God is using it to perfect your faith, to make you stronger, and to improve your character.

Sin grows where some seed has been planted. How you feed your mind determines what seeds you plant in your life. If you plant negative seeds, they will sprout into strong temptation, and if you continue to water them, they will lead to a life of sin. Be aware of the seeds that you plant in your life. Do not let sinful seeds take root and cause you to develop a flesh-pleasing mentality.

The decision to plug in your life creates stronger everyday battles against temptation because winning those battles becomes meaningful in fulfilling God's plan for your life. Every day is filled with battles against temptation that you create with your decision to follow Jesus. If you lose, God will not be upset. In fact, God's Love, Mercy, and Grace will be demonstrated even more in your life as you repent. You have only failed when you give up and surrender your battles by giving in to temptation permanently. When you continue to give a valiant effort to win your daily battles, you are honoring God. God is honored when you don't give up fighting the battles against temptation regardless of how many times you fail. These battles are a test of faith; they are to strengthen your character. The war has already been won by Jesus on the cross—you are forgiven. All you have to do now is give your best effort to win the battles against temptation in your life each day and never give up so that you can experience God's best for your life.

Self-Discipline

For the Spirit God gave us does not make us timid,
but gives us power, love and self-discipline.
—2 Timothy 1:7 NIV

In the 1960's, Stanford University psychology researcher, Walter Mischel conducted a test of self-discipline. He had a group of four-year-olds in a room and put a marshmallow on a plate in front of each of them. He told them that if they could wait fifteen minutes without eating it, then he would give them a second marshmallow. About fourteen years later, Mischel evaluated how those children were doing.

The kids who were able to wait the fifteen minutes for their second marshmallow had more positive attitudes, were more self-motivated, more persistent, and were overall more successful than those who couldn't wait.

The four-year-olds that couldn't wait for the second marshmallow seemed to get into more trouble, were more stubborn, indecisive, unreliable, and had a lower level of self-confidence. Also, they gave in to temptations in their lives more easily.

Many different sources record that those kids who ate their marshmallow immediately at the age of four instead of waiting scored an average of 210 points less on their SAT tests than those who waited for their second marshmallow. A lack of impulse control will lead to a life of frustration and little fulfillment. Self-discipline is necessary to achieve your dreams and accomplish your goals. Without it, you will constantly give in to the temptations of this world and Satan will control many areas of your life.

Self-discipline is the pivotal attribute to your success. It will determine the changes you are able to make in your life, the effectiveness of Brain Matching for you, and also your ability to have patience to trust God in order to overcome life's obstacles.

Like Brain Matching a bad habit, self-discipline is something that will never change unless you make a deliberate effort to change it. You can develop stronger self-discipline by Brain Matching your bad habits through God's Word. You can do this by Brain Matching Bible verses with sin, so when you face sin, you associate it with God's Word against it. If you are persistent, the battle against temptation and resisting short-term pleasure is one that you can win with God every time.

If you are interested in learning more about Walter Mischel's experiment or the development and importance of self-discipline, I recommend his book titled, *The Marshmallow Test: Mastering Self-Control.*

Heaven and Hell

So then, each of us will give an account of ourselves to God.
—Romans 14:12 NIV

Rick Warren explains in *The Purpose Driven Life* (yes, I recommend this book) that God will ask us two questions similar to these when we come before Him after our death on this earth:

1. What did you do with my Son, Jesus Christ?
2. What did you do with what I gave you?

Nobody knows for sure what God will say to you or me when we first see Him, but these two questions seem very reasonable for Him to ask us. The first question simply is just whether you believe in Jesus Christ and made an honest effort to follow His teachings. The second question is referring to the situation that God put you in, the talents that He gave you, the opportunities that He provided you with, and what you did with them in the time that you got. Did you use those things for your own personal glory and pleasure, or did you use them to praise God and fulfill His purpose for your life?

People sometimes get overwhelmed by the concept of Heaven and Hell. It is honestly a simple concept. Those who believe in the resurrection of Jesus and accept God love will spend eternity in Heaven with Him. Those who do not accept God's Love will go to Hell. Heaven is not a motivation, and Hell is not a punishment. If you believe, you are already saved. You don't have to do any work to get to Heaven. In fact, even if you want to, it is impossible to earn a spot in Heaven. Jesus has already done all of the work *for* you. All you have to do is accept that Grace. Instead of Heaven being your motivation, let your life be a response to God's Love. Belief is a call to action, so let Christ's love for you be your motivation to live for Him.

God loves us all unconditionally. The question is, however, what do you do with this love? Do you embrace it or curse God because of it?

Think about someone that you don't particularly like. Would you like to spend eternity in their presence, in their creation? No, obviously you wouldn't, so why would people who hate God in their heart want to spend eternity with Him? Why would people who love sin want to spend eternity in a place free of it?

Josh McDowell wrote in his book, *More Than a Carpenter*, "'How can a loving God allow a sinful individual to go to Hell?' I would ask, 'How can a holy, just, righteous God allow a sinful individual into his presence?'" All God wants is a loving relationship with you. The best way to do that is to read and respond to what He has created—the Bible. The best way to learn about an author is to read his material.

True Disciples

Not everyone who calls out to me, 'LORD! LORD!' will enter the Kingdom of Heaven. Only those who actually do the Will of My Father in heaven will enter. On judgment day many will say to Me, 'LORD! LORD!' We prophesied in Your name and cast out demons in Your name and performed many miracles in Your name. But I will reply, 'I never knew you. Get away from Me, you who break God's Laws.'
—Matthew 7:21-24 NLT

Why Am I Frustrated?

A fish would never be happy living on land, because it was made for water. An eagle could never be satisfied if it wasn't allowed to fly. You will never feel completely satisfied on earth, because you were made for more.
—Rick Warren

We are all fish living on land. That is why life is never fully satisfying to us. When things don't go our way, we get frustrated so easily because we are adding on to our frustration of being out of water.

The earth is not your home; it is just a temporary place to stay. James 4:14 says, *"What is your life? You are a mist that appears for a little while and then vanishes." (NIV)* This life is like a vacation. In 1 Peter 2:11, Peter refers to us as *"temporary residents and foreigners" (NLT)* Your eternal home is in Heaven with Jesus.

Friends, this world is not your home, so don't make yourselves cozy in it. Don't indulge your ego at the expense of your soul.
—1 Peter 2:11 MSG

The material items of this world are meaningless. They will all be gone one day. Records will always be broken, achievements will be forgotten, and eventually trophies will mean nothing. What matters in this life is honoring God by fulfilling His purpose for you and living out of love. Everything else is secondary.

What good will it be for someone to gain the whole world, yet forfeit their soul? Or what can anyone give in exchange for their soul?
—Matthew 16:26 NIV

Some people live for material items. Their goals align with personal wants, and they put themselves in place of God as the one attempting to provide their own fulfillment.

Every one of us does this at some point in some area of our lives. What value do material things have on the eternal scale? To win an award or achieve something that isn't in line with God's purpose for your life is meaningless.

Their destiny is destruction, their god is their stomach, and their glory is in their shame. Their mind is set on earthly things.
—Philippians 3:19 NIV

Remember, you are a fish living on land. One day you will get put back into the water, back home, and you will be able to swim again, free of the struggle, pain, and all of the frustration of this life.

Moral Standard: The Holy Spirit

When the Gentiles sin, they will be destroyed, even though they never had God's written Law. And the Jews, who do have God's Law, will be judged by that Law when they fail to obey it. For merely listening to the Law doesn't make us right with God. It is obeying the Law that makes us right in His sight. Even Gentiles, who do not have God's written Law, show that they know His Law when they instinctively obey it, even without having heard it. They demonstrate that God's Law is written in their hearts, for their own conscience and thoughts either accuse them or tell them they are doing right.
—Romans 2:12-15 NLT

Your moral standard is your natural perception of what is right and what is wrong. It is the Holy Spirit at work within you. In your mind, you are born and raised with moral standard. There isn't a written law that you study every day of your childhood so that you know what is good and what is bad (at least not anymore). You have a natural conception of what is right and wrong because of the moral standard that you are born and raised with.

Why then, if we have a moral standard ingrained in our brains, do we choose to disobey God? We all have a choice of what to do, but we all crave to be repel from authority. Nobody likes to be told what to do, so when we are told what to do, we naturally want to do the opposite.

For example, if a child is told to not eat the candy in the cabinet, what do you think they're going to do? They're going to eat the candy. When we bring attention to temptation, the intensity of that temptation is increased.

We are Heavenly creations on a sinful earth. Therefore, we are all surrounded by constant temptation. We are compelled to do things that are wrong because of the attention that is brought to our sinful nature. What God commands us to do sometimes doesn't look as sweet as the short-term pleasures of this world because our lives aren't plugged into God's eternity perspective. Temptation is strong when you look at things with an earthly perspective, but God has a Heavenly perspective. He is our guidance home—our Savior.

When you plug in your life, temptation starts to fade because your moral standard is enhanced, and the importance of God's Word is realized. When we are unplugged and disconnected from God, sometimes all we see Jesus' teachings as are rules telling us how to live *our* lives. We take God's Word as a suggestion because we can't see the whole picture. We are living meaningless life as an unplugged computer or dead phone. When you plug in your life, Jesus' teachings become a blessing, and you *want* to learn and apply them.

When you grow up, you have to do what your parents tell you to do. Why? Because it is what you required to do. The last thing a kid wants to do is clean their room, make their bed, and wash the dishes. They will complain about it, and refuse at times because they don't see a purpose in doing it. However, as a child grows and is pushed by their parents to continually do the same chores, the child will begin to see the impact of what they do and learn that they are making a difference and helping out. As the child grows and gets older, they might even offer to help their parents with extra things because they actually begin to *want* to help out, and they see the purpose in what they do. This is the same with you and your relationship with Jesus. He teaches you certain things to do that you may not like or see as useful to you, but when you realize that living by God's Will is the only fulfilling way to live, you will begin to trust Him with everything He tells you to do, and you will want to do what He says because you want His full plan for your life.

You know that your life is starting to be plugged in when you feel sorrowful with each sin—not sorrowful about disobeying God necessarily, but abashed that you robbed yourself of a divine opportunity. When that starts happening, you know that you are on the right path. Sorrow over sin is not a bad feeling because it shows yourself that you care about God's Will and have a want for it in your life.

But if I know that what I am doing is wrong, this
shows that I agree that the Law is good.
—Romans 7:16 NLT

Paul says in 2 Corinthians 7:10, *"For the kind of sorrow God wants us to experience leads us away from sin and results in salvation. There's no regret for that kind of sorrow. But worldly sorrow, which lacks repentance, results in spiritual death."* (NLT) God has created this feeling of sorrow due to sin in order to help aid you in repentance. You know the Holy Spirit is becoming more of a factor in your life when this sorrow for sin becomes more apparent.

Your moral standard produced by the Holy Spirit within you is what guides you to follow the Will of God. In Acts 26:14, Paul is in court before King Agrippa and Festus telling about his conversion and says, "*We all fell to the ground, and I heard a voice saying to me in Aramaic, 'Saul, Saul, why do you persecute me? It is hard for you to kick against the goads.'"* (NIV)

"Goads" are long sticks with a pointed tip used to startle cattle when they get out of line. They are designed for farmers to more effectively move the cattle where they want them to go. The New Living Translation replaces "the goads" with "My Will." God is the farmer, and we are His cattle. He is moving us wherever He wants us to go because

He knows what is best for us. He knows that if we wander off, we will not get to the place that we need to go in order to live the way He intends us to. When you feel the Holy Spirit startling you before you take action or make a decision, remember that God knows better than you do. It is hard for you to fight the Holy Spirit—"It is hard for you to kick against the goads." Fighting God's Will can cause us to have a feeling of regret once we realize that we are lost, but the Father will always look for you and find you if you manage to wander off. Matthew 18:12-13 is *The Parable of the Wandering Sheep*:

> *"What do you think? If a man owns a hundred sheep, and one of them wanders away, will He not leave the ninety-nine on the hills and go to look for the one that wandered off? And if He finds it, truly I tell you, He is happier about that one sheep than about the ninety-nine that did not wander off."*

You are God's prized possession. If you wonder off, He will look for you, and when He finds you—when you turn to Him—He will be happier than ever before. God, the Farmer, is taking you where you need to go.

Every good tree bears good fruit, but a bad tree bears bad fruit.
—Matthew 7:17 NIV

When you plug in your life and embrace the Holy Spirit within you, you will start to produce good fruit. The things that you do will begin to have meaning and purpose. When you let God have complete control of your life, your life starts to become fulfilling and joy that you didn't think existed in this sinful world rushes into your life through the cords that come out of the outlet.

11

Life

There was once a man who was picking berries for his family in the woods. As he was looking for the berries, a ferocious tiger jumped out and started to chase him across a field. At the edge of the field, there was a cliff. In order to escape the jaws of the tiger, the man caught hold of a vine and swung himself over the edge of the cliff. Dangling down, he saw, to his dismay, there were more tigers on the ground below him! And, furthermore, two little mice were gnawing on the vine to which he clung. He knew that at any moment he would fall to certain death. That's when he noticed a wild strawberry growing in a tiny hole on the cliff wall. Clutching the vine with one hand, he plucked the strawberry with the other and put it in his mouth.

My football coach told us this story before the last home game of the season one year. The story is summarized from an old Zen Tale called, *The Strawberry Story*. When I heard it, it really resonated with me. He said that no matter what's going on around you, take this moment and enjoy it: "Let tonight be your strawberry."

In life, you will always have *strawberry moments*. Bad things happen, and everyone has their own struggles in life. I understand that you are surrounded by stress, disappointment, fear, and a lot of negative feelings in this world. However, what you have right now is a simple strawberry in the midst of everything—this moment.

God gave you this life to enjoy. He wants you to smile. He wants you to learn to enjoy each moment with the realization that this world is not your home. Enjoy the strawberries of your life.

Then Jesus explained: "My nourishment comes from doing the Will of God, who sent me, and from finishing His work."
—John 4:34 NLT

Living in Response to Love

The Romans were masters at whipping someone to the verge of death. This is what they did to Jesus. He then carried a 125-pound pabulum (the horizontal piece of the cross) on His lacerated back up Via Dolarosa, or "The Way of Suffering" to be nailed to a cross with 7-9 inch nails. He hung there in agony for six hours. In those six hours while Jesus was on the cross, *you* were all He thought about.

If this act of love doesn't call you to action, nothing will. Stop living with a sense of condemnation. God loves you and has a plan for your life. What's stopping you from giving it all up to Him? Plug in your life.

Afterword

Knowing is not enough, we must apply.
Willing is not enough, we must do.
—*Bruce Lee*

My hope for you is that you apply all of the principles in this book to your life. I hope that by applying them, they start to enhance your life and outlook on what you are doing and who you are. Life is hard, and it's not as simple as words sometimes make it, but if you are *willing* to change and you *want* to change, then you can *definitely* change.

What I want for this book is for it to help turn your life in a direction where you are willingly letting God work through you and enhance the way you live. From that point, and only from that point, will you develop into who you were truly made to be, live your life with purpose and conviction with your eternal purpose in mind, and ultimately live a fulfilling life.

I hope that this book has guided you to love who you are and love your life. Love is very powerful, and love is the basis of this book because everything in life is controlled by the central source of love—God. He is love Himself, and we are made in His image, therefore we must love each other and live out of love in order to live the way that we are made to.

I apply many of the principles in this book to my own life, and they all have a huge impact on how I live. Embracing and applying these principles is a commitment that might take some time. Maybe you are ready to plug in your life now, or maybe you need to pray for guidance to find your path to a plugged in relationship with your God. Plugging in your life and choosing to live your life entirely God's way is a decision that you have to make on your own. Nobody can plug your life in for you. People might support you and aid you in doing it, as this book has shown you, but ultimately it's your life and your journey with God, so plugging in your life must be your own decision.

I hope that this book expands your faith and propels you in a direction to make the most of each moment in your life. Follow your goals and dreams. Each day is a blessing, so treat it that way and live with a sense of hope. My prayer for you is that you are inspired by the words of this book and that you will use them as guidance to follow your meaningful goals and dreams, God's way.

Plug in your life and let God's Joy, Mercy, Grace, Purpose, Love, and perfect Will rush through the cords as eternity volts into your life.

'Father, if You are willing, please take this cup of suffering away from me. ***Yet I want Your Will to be done, not mine.'***

—Luke 22:42 NLT

Acknowledgements

I would like to thank my family for always supporting me along the way in everything that I do. I love you all, and you are all so very important to me. I'd do anything for any one of you. You inspire me every single day, and I hope that this book dramatically influences your lives as it has done to me in the process of writing it. I hope that you guys really apply the principles that are in this book to your lives. Our family is not average. We are a special family, we always build each other up, and I am excited for all of the achievements that every one of us continues to have.

I'd particularly like to point out a few people who were very influential in the making of this book:

Mom and dad, the writing and publishing of his book could not have happened without you. Thank you for your constant support in the process of writing and publishing this book and for helping me to make this dream come true. You amaze me, and I hope that one day I can have a marriage as strong and happy as yours and inspire my children in the same way you inspire me. You both let me be myself and help me to grow every single day in every area of my life. You let me be close to God and provide me with all that I need. You guys are amazing, and I cannot express how much I love you both.

Logan, you never doubted me through the writing and publishing of this book, and you supported me in the process. Throughout my whole life, I've learned so much from you, and I look up to you as a role model, and I always will. You inspire me to never settle for average. You're my best friend. I love how you do things your own way despite how everyone else does them around you.

Mara and Sadie, you guys aren't old enough to really understand this book yet, but one day you will be, and I hope that it is something that both of you live by. I hope you both choose to follow God's plan for your life. You both inspire me every day by your love for me. I hope that you guys develop a best friend relationship as Logan and I did. Mara, I love your generosity. Sadie, I love your uniqueness.

Grandma and papa, you guys are always supporting all of your grandchildren's goals and dreams. You teach me so many lessons about life, both of you, and it means so much to me to have such incredible grandparents. All of your grandchildren recognize all that you do for them and are grateful for the love that you give us all. You are both full of love, and I would be so blessed if I could be like you when I grow older. Thank you so much for all of your inspiration, not only by your words but by your actions as well. You are both perfect examples of people who live out of love. I love you both so much, and I love your hearts.

Ian, you have always supported me in everything that I aspire to do, and I will always be here for you to be transparent with, to share ideas with, and hold you accountable to your goals and dreams. We will always do great things together, and I'm excited for what the future has to bring. Thank you for all of your inspiration and honesty that you provide me with. I love your burning motivation.

Thank you so much Madeline. Every time I see you, I light up with excitement. You are so incredible and will do great things because of your dedication and perseverance. You have inspired me so much over the years, and I hope that you got a lot out of this book. I love our conversations and the relationship that we have. You are the "mighty girl" forever. I love your consistency Mads.

Kaitlynn, you knew all along that I was writing this book and were always excited to hear how it was coming. Who you are and your consistent perseverance through all of life's adversity inspires me in such a dramatic way. I love sharing my ideas with you and hearing yours. Thank you for aiding me in developing into the person that I am today. I love your perseverance and strength.

I'd like to thank Mr. Gernovich, Tony, Mr. Johnson, Mr. Hotchkiss, Mr. Priestap, Pastor Kelly, and the members and staff at McLane Church for all that they have taught me and their continual guidance. Kyle Idleman, Craig Groeschel, Eric Thomas, Joel Osteen, and Dave Stone, thank you as well for inspiring me to follow the path that I am on today. Thank you to all of my coaches and teachers along the way. Thank you coach Root, coach Wilbur, coach Moneta, coach Peyton, coach Patton and Killian, and thank you coach Banks. A couple of teachers that I would like to particularly thank are Mrs. Williams, Dr. Tong, Mr. Mattocks, Mrs. Palmer, Mrs. White, Mrs. Zurad, Mr. Byers, Mr. Smrekar, and Mrs. Irwin.

Thank you West Bow Press publishing company. Thank you for your commitment to making my book the best it could possibly be.

Thank you, Trese. You have taught me so much about writing and made me realize how much it actually means to be an author. You introduced me to many new things to think about when I write that will help me in the future. Without you, this book would not be even close to as great as it is. Thank you for being critical of my ideas but supportive as well. You have made me a better writer and a deeper thinker.

My final thank you is to Jesus, my Lord and Savior. He has given me so many great gifts—writing being a very special one. I am very excited for what He will do in my life next.

This book started off as a dream, but because of the Grace of God and the supporting relationships that I have, my dream was made into a reality for His glory. I hope that you enjoyed this book and the hard work that was put into it. I also hope that you make the decision to live a plugged in life and begin to experience all that God has in store for you.

Notes

1. "BibleGateway." *.com: A Searchable Online Bible in over 100 Versions and 50 Languages*. N.p., n.d. Web. 17 July 2015.
2. Szalavitz, Maia, and Maia Szalavitz. "The Secrets of Self-Control: The Marshmallow Test 40 Years Later | TIME.com." *Time*. Time, n.d. Web. 4 February 2015.
3. "Read and Study the Bible Online - Search, Find Verses." *Bible Study Tools*. N.p., n.d. Web. 17 July 2015.
4. "Fears We Are Born with | Thought Provokers." *Fears We Are Born with | Thought Provokers*. N.p., n.d. Web. 27 December 2014.
5. "Hate." *Hate*. N.p., n.d. Web. 1 July 2015.

Printed in the United States
By Bookmasters